Make Mine a Martini

Make Mine a Martini

Kay Plunkett-Hogge

Photography by Kate Whitaker

MITCHELL BEAZLEY

For Fred.

My chief barman, who stirs and shakes me always.

CONTENTS

INTRODUCTION

Let me begin by saying this: **I'm not a bartender, but I've known a few.** And I don't own a bar, but I've been to my fair share. I've stolen the keys to the Formosa, danced at the Bamboo Bar, frolicked at The Frolic Room, fallen backwards off my stool at Odeon, and behaved with perfect English rectitude while supping Claridge's finest Martini. So I like to think I've picked up a thing or two about drinks and snacks, not all of it by osmosis.

And if there's one thing I've learned, it's that the cocktail isn't just for when you're 'out'. **There's nothing better at the end of the week than a crisp Martini to round things off.** It's better still with a couple of snacks. And, even better than that, *in the company of friends.*

From my earliest days, *I've always loved a cocktail party.* They were a constant feature of my Bangkok childhood. I remember clambering on to my chest of drawers when I was small, and peering out though the shutters to see what all the chattering and laughter was about. There was my mum, looking glamorous in a slinky silk dress; there was Dad, looking smooth in shirtsleeves and skinny trousers; and there were the couples twisting on the terracotta-tiled terrace, everyone sipping cocktails and spearing snacks with sticks. It was convivial, content and oh, so relaxed. And it's left me with a hankering for those **happy days and nights.**

So, in this book, I've gathered together some classic cocktails with a few of my own inventions, and added a selection of canapés which are **easy to make at home** and a few tips to make a cocktail party that little bit easier. After all, just the sound of ice being shaken, preferably to a rhythm all of its own, is enough to **bring a smile to anyone's face.** It's the promise of sweet relief, of good times, good friends and good conversation. *Just make mine a Martini.*

 A little green cocktail fork next to a photo indicates there is a recipe for the drink or dish shown in the picture on another page.

A little red cocktail fork next to a recipe will lead you to a photo of the drink or dish in question.

Before we begin

A good party can be rigorously planned or entirely impromptu — it all depends on the occasion. But here are a few key things to get us started.

HOME BAR BASICS

Setting up a bar at home needn't be an expensive undertaking. At the very least, you only really need something to mix in and a glass for your drink (I've used a clean coffee pot to stir a Martini before now – it's not glamorous, but it works). But there are a few things that will make your life easier.

1 A GOOD SHAKER

This is really a matter of preference. You want something that fits comfortably in your hand when you shake it, and which has a tight fit when it's closed (there's nothing worse than scrubbing Daiquiris off the ceiling, let me tell you). Some people favour the Boston Shaker, with its metal base and slightly smaller glass mixing top. I prefer a compact all-metal shaker, known as a Cobbler Shaker, which has a built-in strainer. Mine makes 2–3 cocktails at a time and fits nicely into my rather small hands.

The French Shaker lacks the Cobbler's strainer and, again, is an all-metal affair. I think the metal matters. Although I have a couple of beautiful glass shakers, I keep them purely for decoration (along with my 1930s bear-shaped Cobbler Shaker, which is entirely impractical, but which makes me laugh). The conductivity of metal chills the drink quicker and with less dilution.

2 A STRAINER

This is vital if you lack a Cobbler Shaker, because you generally want to strain a drink into a glass. They come in fairly standard sizes to fit easily over the mouths of most shakers. Often, you'll find them in a set with a cocktail shaker and a jigger. Just make sure, when you buy one, that it's well made: the cheap ones can be a bit loose where the handle meets the circle of the strainer, and they have a tendency to nip your skin.

3 A BAR SPOON

A bar spoon is a very long teaspoon – as a measure, they're identical – with a fat, flattened end which you can use to crush things like sugar cubes. In a bar, they're very handy. Do you need one at home? Probably not. But you do need…

4 A MUDDLER

…an elongated wooden pestle for crushing the oils out of leaves, breaking sugar into bitters and so on. When it comes to muddling leaves, wood is always better than metal – it's gentler and less bruising, preserving the leaf's integrity while extracting the flavours you require for the drink. In an emergency, the handle of a wooden spoon will do.

5 A JIGGER

If you want something to taste right, measurements matter. In the UK, cocktail measures are based on the standard bar measures as laid down by law for the sale of spirits (25 ml for a single, 50 ml for a double in England and Wales; 35 ml and 70 ml in Scotland), and most jiggers and measurers sold there conform to these standards. In the US, cocktails are generally measured by the fluid ounce, which works out at approximately 30 ml for a single shot, and 60 ml for a double. On page 22, I have listed cocktails that dance to the 1:1:2 rhythm or similar, and upscale easily by ratio. It doesn't really matter whether you use a US or a UK measure for these, so long as you stick to the same one. I favour a glass measurer or jigger with measurements marked in both millilitres and fluid ounces on the side.

6 A JUICER

If you're planning to make Margaritas or Daiquiris for a party, trust me, you want some kind of electric citrus juicer. It saves an awful lot of time and effort. And it will also allow you to squeeze fresh orange or grapefruit juice for breakfast. That's a win in anyone's book.

7 A BLENDER

There are only a couple of drinks in this book which use a blender, and, to be honest, you could shake them if you have to. However, I find my KitchenAid Artisan Blender indispensible: a good blender allows you to whip up frozen drinks, blend fruit juices and so on. Plus it's good for making soup – and what's soup if not a hot, non-alcoholic cocktail?

8 A KILLER BLACK DRESS

Or a sharp suit. Obviously.

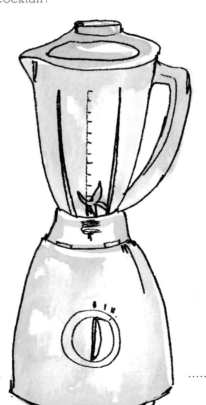

SPIRITS

It goes without saying that, without spirits, there are no cocktails. Apart from the non-alcoholic ones on pages 130–43. In this book, I have deliberately tried not to prescribe certain brands in favour of others, but there are a few instances where the recipes have to be specific. For example, a Zombie is not a Zombie without Bacardi 151, and that's all there is to it. But, by and large, buying should be determined by the following points:

1 **Quality matters,** regardless of those who claim (wrongly) that cocktails were invented to hide the deficiencies in Prohibition-era booze. Buy the best you can afford.

2 **Buy the brands you like.** This cannot be said enough. People spout a lot of blether about booze and wine, particularly

about wine, but there is one golden rule: if you like it, it's good. To hell with the pedants and snobs. There's not a huge amount of difference between various brands of vodka (and any vodka can be improved by a pass through a bleached coffee filter paper), but when you look

at gins in particular, there's so much variation that you have to try a few to pick your favourite. I lean towards Beefeater and, for a change, Plymouth or Sipsmith, but that's not to speak against Tanqueray, Hendrick's or Bombay Sapphire, or any of the others, for that matter.

When it comes to rum you should note that, beyond quality, different rums provide different flavours. White rums are distinct from amber and dark rums while aged rums and rhums agricole are different again. It's worth experimenting to find the ones you like – like wine regions, different countries produce distinct products, and there's lots to explore.

The same goes for whisky. Ryes and bourbons have subtly different characters. So, too, do Scotch whisky and Irish whiskey – they even spell the word differently! But, while quality is important in a cocktail, it's a crime to mix anything with a good malt whisky. Those that have have been found bludgeoned to death with tam o'shanters in dim back alleys. You've been warned.

3 **Space.** Most of us don't have room for a lot of bottles, so buy for the cocktails you make most often.

VERMOUTH

Every bar needs a sweet vermouth and a dry vermouth, depending on the drinks you favour. As a fortified wine, it keeps for a while, though it does deteriorate slowly over time, so keep open bottles in the fridge. I favour Noilly Prat for a dry vermouth and Martini for sweet, and I'm a big fan of the Cocchi di Torino range for their extraordinary character and flair. Try a few different brands (ideally in other people's bars) to find the ones you like.

BITTERS

Bitters lift and distinguish a cocktail. Often, they turn out to be the secret ingredient which makes a drink sing. These days, a lot of bartenders make their own from wildly diverse ingredients. You absolutely, categorically need a bottle of Angostura bitters in your bar. It will last for ages, and it is highly adaptable. But if you have room, a bottle of orange bitters will always come in handy, as will some Peychaud's bitters from New Orleans. And one of my favourite bitters companies, The Bitter Truth, makes a very handy five-bottle travel box – the celery bitters within makes for an excellent Bloody Mary.

GARNISHES

The peel of citrus fruits used to make twists should always be unwaxed. One bartender I know makes an Essence of Sex Wax, which is used for greasing surf boards but, beyond that, I can see no earthly reason for wax to come anywhere near a cocktail. The wax on citrus fruits may help their preservation, but it hinders the release of the oils in their peel which, when we use a twist, is what we're after. Speaking of which, if you want to add a touch of fancy, squeeze the oils through a lit match or lighter. They will ignite and caramelize in the flame, which makes for a lovely aroma, particularly in an Old Fashioned.

Make sure you have a sharp knife, or a channel knife, and a chopping board for prepping all kinds of citrus and other fruit. Though, to be honest, when it's just me, I often cut a twist of citrus with a potato peeler…

While we're on the subject of garnishes, look out for good quality maraschino cherries. Luxardo, who make a fine maraschino liqueur, sell the real thing in jars. I recommend them.

SUGAR SYRUP

You can buy sugar syrup in bottles, but it is very easy to make at home and considerably cheaper. Simply measure out equal quantities of caster (superfine) sugar and water, say 250 ml (8 fl oz) of water to 250 g (8 oz) of sugar, into a saucepan. Then dissolve the sugar completely in the water over a low heat (the heat isn't strictly necessary, it just speeds up the process). Allow the mixture to cool, then store the sugar syrup in a sterilized bottle for up to a month in the fridge.

BAR STYLE

There's no excuse for not having **a stylish bar.** It's the perfect place to reflect your taste. Scour the internet, charity shops and flea markets to find quirky glasses, plates, napkins and cocktail forks to customize yours.

SIZE DOES MATTER...

...when it comes to glasses. I am a little obsessed with collecting small Martini glasses which hold, traditionally, a gulp or three, so you can drink that chilly charmer while it is still suitably cold. *(If you see any, do get in touch...)*

Make sure that you have the right glass for the right drink, size-wise at least. This is not Big Gulp time at the drive through. It's the cocktail hour... At all costs avoid those ridiculous bucket-like glasses that should really only be sold at novelty stores for keeping marbles, goldfish or small coins in. Anything but a cocktail.

SHAKEN VS. STIRRED

This is really about ice. Ice and dilution. When you shake a cocktail, you break the ice cubes, leaving tiny shards of ice in the drink. These shards dilute the drink, balancing the flavours in a shaken cocktail. When you stir, this dilution is commensurately less.

Since ice both chills and weakens a cocktail (chilling is good, weakening less so…), there are a few things to keep in mind to make sure you get the best from it.

1 The more ice you put in the shaker, the faster it will chill a drink, shaken or stirred, with less dilution. With a shaker, more ice is better.

2 The size of an ice cube matters: the smaller the ice cubes, the more surface area there is to melt into the drink. Which is why many bartenders will serve drinks like an Old Fashioned with a single large ice cube to minimize the dilution.

3 Over time, ice picks up the flavours of other things in your freezer. You should always make sure you have fresh ice when you make cocktails – there's nothing worse than a hint of old dinners in your Gimlet.

Shaking and stirring give you control over the sharpness of the alcohol in a cocktail. When it comes to a drink like a Martini, it is as ever a question of preference. So try it both ways and find out which you prefer. So long as your cocktail's cold!

BAR SNACKS

Every good drink, and indeed every good drinks party, needs a toothsome accompaniment. Snacks, canapés, eats: call them what you will. So on pages 144–219 are some of my favourites, things I find my guests love and that do not take me away from them for too long.

To be honest, you could totally ignore the recipe section and just trot along to your nearest deli to buy a gorgeous selection of cheese, charcuterie and olives. Maybe even a paté or a pie. Or throw out some nuts; I wouldn't hold it against you. Some of my favourite bar snacks of all time are the monkey nuts in their shells at Chez Jay in Santa Monica. They arrive in a red plastic basket, you just pop them open and discard the shells on the floor. Chez Jay's owner, Jay Fiondella famously persuaded Alan Shepard to take one of them to the moon and back – the very first astro-nut! (If you're out that way, pop in for a visit and one of their fine Margaritas.)

THE ART OF THE PARTY

Throwing a good party should be enormous fun, both for your guests and for you.
Here are some simple tips to help things go with a swing.

DRINKS

It doesn't matter how many people you've
invited, the fact of it is that you don't run a
bar. You don't have every kind of liquor or
elixir stuffed into a cupboard, so the whole
gamut of cocktails is out of the question.
Offer a couple of options, and wine and
beer if you feel like it. If you have a large
number of guests, by which I mean more
than 20, it's a good idea to choose a drink
you can scale up and premix.

SCALING UP

A lot of cocktail recipes can be
restructured so that you think about their
ingredients in terms of ratios instead of
measurements. This makes it very much
easier to scale them up for a party. The
Margarita (see page 78) works out as one
part lime juice to one part triple sec to two
parts tequila (1:1:2). So before anyone
arrives, your can premix a perfect batch of
cocktails to those proportions, beginning

with the ingredient of which you have the least (which is usually the lime juice), and then shake them over ice for your guests as required. Here are some cocktails that scale up beautifully:

- The Margarita (see page 78)
- The Cosmopolitan (see page 51) – just add the dash of cranberry as you shake each one
- The Classic Daiquiri (see page 105)
- Tom's April Sour (see page 43)
- The Fine and Dandy (see page 40)
- The Classic Rum Punch (see page 91)

FOOD

Again, keep it simple. Never forget that your friends have come round to see you, so it's not going to be the ideal evening if you never leave the kitchen! The snacks need to be substantial enough to stop people from feeling the effects of the cocktails TOO much. And they need to go with the setting – if it's an evening where everyone's on their feet, you want food that's easy to hold and isn't going to drip down somebody's frock. If it's a smaller affair, or a brunch, then plates and forks (oh, how I do love a cocktail fork!) can come out, and the food can be a little more robust.

The important thing is to make sure you serve things that reflect the numbers you've invited. The more people, the simpler you want it to be. If there are just eight of you, then you might want to cook a few things that take a bit of time. If there are 28, you'd probably prefer to serve something less arduous to prepare. So choose your canapés accordingly.

HOW MUCH IS ENOUGH?

Here are a few tips to make the question of how much to feed and water the masses a little easier:

- For wine, half a bottle of wine or bubbly per person is fairly standard. But I have a deep-set fear of running out, so I always veer towards three-quarters to a bottle per person, and know I'll have leftovers. Most wine merchants will sell wine by the case on sale or return. Just be careful not to ice all the white wine or Champagne because they won't accept it back if you soak off the labels.

- I generally estimate two to three cocktails an hour per head, plus one for luck! Bear in mind that most people will slow down as the evening goes on.

- Always have plenty of still and sparkling water on hand and at least one non-alcoholic drink.

- If the party is to last two hours, bank on 8–10 canapés per head, of perhaps 3–5 different types.
- For three hours, go for 12–14 canapés per head, of perhaps 6–8 different types.
- For four hours plus – well, at this point you can echo my father: 'I invited you for drinks, not breakfast.' At which point he'd ring a large ship's bell. You can just smile and say the party is over.
- If you are serving pre-dinner drinks, however, I think 4–5 canapés per head is fine: you want them to have room for their dinner! In fact, I often just serve Salted Almonds (see page 33) and a Soup Shot (see pages 148–51) if we're heading into a substantial meal.

PLANNING

This is what it all comes down to. The more you can prepare ahead of time, the easier your evening will be. For a start, you'll feel more relaxed and so will your friends. The problem is that so many of us suffer from performance anxiety when it comes to entertaining and, really, we shouldn't. After all, everyone you've invited is meant to be a friend, so what can go wrong?

So let's shake up some cocktails and stir up some trouble. After all, it's meant to be a party!

BEFORE, DURING & AFTER THE EVENT

I don't want to preach, but here are a few tips that I've found invaluable.

1 Make sure you take into account who you're inviting and why. If it's a party to welcome your new boss it's going to be a very different affair to one that marks the start of the football season. Extreme comparisons I know, but you get the drift.

2 Casting: don't invite two feuding ex-lovers, especially to a smaller affair. Likewise anyone you know who, God forbid, is a mean drunk. Bigger parties have less issues as everyone can mix and mingle without ruffling feathers.

3 Unless you intend on hiring extra help, I wouldn't advise going much above the 25–30 guest mark at home. You want to enjoy yourself rather than plan a military exercise!

4 Do enlist family and friends to help: most people love to be useful.

5 Regardless of the occasion, make sure you invite your guests in a timely fashion. I don't mean sending an official embossed card posted months before the event, but three weeks' notice is good. It gives you enough time to get organized too. If you want to have a dress code, make sure they know in advance to avoid embarrassment. Ask if they have any dietary needs or allergies.

6 Will people be driving? While your guests' sobriety is not (entirely) your responsibility, I think it's a courtesy to make sure there's a solid non-alcoholic alternative if you know people are coming by car. And do supply phone numbers for local taxi services, too.

7 Think about whether you need to rent glasses and plates. Have the liquor delivered, too, if you can, to save time.

8 Ice, ice, baby… Make sure there's PLENTY of it. Have some tubs (or baby baths) at the ready to receive it!

9 Décor – or un-décor: If you've invited more than a handful of guests, then think about clearing some space for food, for drinks, for shimmying and mingling. Pop away anything that's fragile or precious… or precarious. And beware of lit candles when the drinks are flowing.

10 Make it VERY clear whether there are smoking areas or not.

11 Fresh flowers, space and a smile are the best decoration. If you are doing Margaritas and tacos, some bright colours and patterns may add a touch of tropical heat. But I tend to advise against 'themes'. It's a party, not a party game.

12 Don't forget to HOST! If everyone there already knows everyone else – then fine, things can take care of themselves. If not, well, I know you'll be busy, but make sure you introduce people. It's the one thing everyone forgets, and it's the one thing that makes sure everyone has a good time. If you see someone alone in the corner while you're busy frying Arancini, send a gregarious friend over to help them mingle.

After the event: don't wash the glasses until the morning (BR-EAK-AGE!!) That tip's from my wonderful mama!

The Drinks

So here we are, at the main course – if a drink can be a main course. Here's everything from the Americano to the Zombie. Take your pick. And mix.

GIN
THE MARTINI

The food writer MFK Fisher once said that the Martini is to America what vodka is to Russia. Hemingway said they made him feel civilized. I say they are the perfect antidote to rainy days (literally or figuratively) – to quote Mae West, I like to get out of my wet clothes and into a dry Martini. **No other cocktail inspires more comment or opinion.** Should it be shaken? Should it be stirred? Should it be gin or should it be vodka? And how much vermouth is too much vermouth?

Throwing myself into the Martini melee, I should point out that the opinions below are merely my own. They're also right. So don't argue.

Shaken or stirred is a matter of preference. I prefer mine stirred to the point where it's as cold as the bottom of a penguin's foot. If you shake it, you will break the ice cubes and make a cloudy and more diluted drink. I think that a Martini's ice-cold clarity is a big part of its charm.

A Martini is made with gin. A Vodka Martini is made with vodka. Apple Martinis are an abomination. That is all.

An olive or a twist is also a matter of preference, *but the twist should always be lemon* – if you want lime, order a Gimlet and be done with it. The lemon should be unwaxed. The olive should be vividly green and unstuffed. If you like it 'dirty' – with a splash of the olive brine – be as dirty as you please.

Salted Almonds
see page 33

'I like to get out of my wet clothes and into a dry Martini'

MAE WEST

I don't care that Noel Coward thought it sufficient to wave the shaker in the general direction of Italy – **there must be vermouth.** So you can add a drop of vermouth to your gin with a pipette, you can swirl the vermouth through the glass and discard it (the Bartender's Martini, as seen at The Frolic Room), or you can be like Clark Gable's Jim Gannon in *Teacher's Pet*, and simply wet the vermouth cork and wipe it around the rim of your Martini glass. This is a mixed drink:

without the vermouth, it's not a Martini. It's just a glass of cold gin.

The ice must be fresh. The longer it's in your freezer, the more it picks up residual flavours. With the Martini, we're shooting for drinking perfection. We'll never make it, but we were born to try.

This is how I make mine...

Fill a cocktail shaker with fresh ice. Pour in one-eighth of a cap of dry vermouth – we're talking about ¼ teaspoon. I favour Noilly Prat. Stir vigorously to coat the ice cubes thoroughly. Add a cocktail-glassful of gin. Or two, or three, if you're making more, though I never make more than three in one batch as the drink becomes too diluted before it reaches the requisite temperature. Stir until it's as cold as a corrupted politician's soul. Leave to rest for a minute or two while you spear your olives on to a cocktail stick or cut your lemon twist. Strain into the glass, garnish and serve at once, ideally with Salted Almonds (see right).

Note: Apart from those made at 91a, the best Martinis I believe are made by the ever-young Manny Aguirre at The Musso and Frank Grill in Hollywood. He is, indeed, The Merlin of Martinis.

SALTED ALMONDS

If you don't do anything else at all, just make these. There is nothing like a salted almond with a dry Martini. Heaven.

200 g (7 oz) blanched almonds

½ tsp softened unsalted butter

fine sea salt

Preheat the oven to 140°C/275°F/Gas Mark 1. Place the almonds on a baking sheet and, with your hands, generously coat them all over with the butter.
   Bake for 25–30 minutes, checking every now and then and giving them a shake, until they are honey blonde.
   Remove from the oven and place straight on to a sheet of greaseproof paper. Salt them generously straight away. Then crumple up the paper a little and leave to cool. Transfer to a bowl, sprinkle with the salt left on the paper and serve.

Note: For more nut recipes, see page 179.

For a picture of this recipe,
see page 31

I FLIP FOR FELICITY

When my dear friend and agent Felicity got married, we asked what she'd like for a present. 'Well,' she said, 'I could use a drink.' This is it.

The flip is arguably the oldest of cocktails, and certainly among the first of the American classics, combining spirit and egg with sugar and spice. We've lightened this one, removing the egg yolk, and sharpened it up with a little lemon. *And, with its hint of English rose, need I say more?*

50 ml (1¾ fl oz) gin

25 ml (¾ fl oz) fresh lemon juice

1 egg white

15 ml (½ fl oz) sugar syrup (see page 17)

5 ml (1 tsp) rose water

a good dash of Angostura bitters

Pour the gin, lemon juice, egg white, syrup, rose water and bitters into a cocktail shaker. Shake hard to emulsify. Fill with ice and shake until very cold, then strain into a cocktail glass. It should be frothy, with a slight blush, and delightfully cold.

KAY'S TIP: The qualities of rose water vary enormously. You need a pure rose water for this — if you only have one made with concentrate, use just a drop, otherwise the drink will taste too much like Turkish Delight.

THE VESPER

This is the classic cocktail of Bond, named for Vesper Lynd, the chic femme fatale of *Casino Royale* (oh, to make one's entrance in a dress of black velvet, 'simple and yet with a touch of splendour that only half a dozen couturiers in the world can achieve'!). In the book it's made with gin, vodka and Kina Lillet, a fortified wine bittered with quinine. Lillet modernized it in the 1980s to make Lillet Blanc, which is less bitter, and some bartenders now use Cocchi Aperitivo Americano to attain the original flavour. *I think that touch of bitterness is appropriately Bond-esque.* He may have named a drink after her, but it can't ease the hurt of her betrayal. I like to think that in 'the violet hour', an older Bond might order one and remember Vesper a little more kindly.

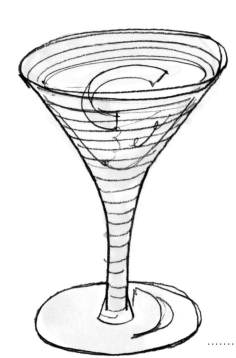

60 ml (2 fl oz) gin

20 ml (¾ fl oz) vodka

10 ml (2 tsp) Lillet Blanc or Cocchi Aperitivo Americano

a large twist of lemon, to garnish

Fill a cocktail shaker with ice and pour in the gin, vodka and Lillet Blanc. Shake vigorously until it's ice cold. Then strain into a Martini glass and garnish with a large, thin twist of lemon peel.

Note: Bond says Gordon's gin; I prefer something with 40 per cent alcohol.

'When I'm…er…concentrating,' says Bond, 'I never like to have more than one drink before dinner. But I do like that one to be large and very strong and very cold and very well-made.' Well… this *is* strong, and arguably enough for two ordinary mortals lacking in Bond's super-human capacity for alcohol!

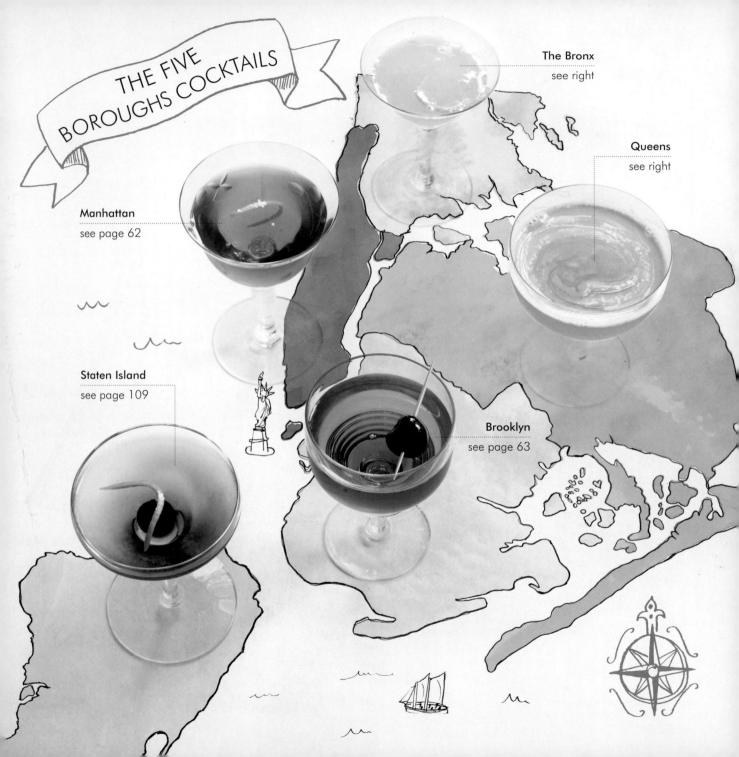

THE FIVE BOROUGHS COCKTAILS

The Bronx
see right

Queens
see right

Manhattan
see page 62

Staten Island
see page 109

Brooklyn
see page 63

THE BRONX

One of the Five Boroughs Cocktails, this drink was allegedly created by Bronx-born restaurateur Joseph Sormani in Philadelphia around 1905. Its proportions vary from recipe to recipe, ranging from equal parts of gin and the two vermouths with just a dash of orange juice and orange bitters, **to the much drier version I use here.** The Bronx also exists in silver and gold versions – the silver contains an egg white, and the gold an egg yolk. If you fancy either version, make sure you shake it vigorously *before* you add the ice so that it emulsifies properly, then shake again.

15 ml (½ fl oz) fresh orange juice

10 ml (2 tsp) red vermouth

10 ml (2 tsp) dry vermouth

40 ml (1¼ fl oz) gin

a twist of orange, to garnish

Fill a cocktail shaker with ice and add the orange juice, vermouths and the gin. Shake until it's very cold, then strain into a Martini glass and garnish with a twist of orange. Serve at once.

THE QUEENS

This is apparently a genuine Harry Craddock cocktail, or so says Robert Vermeire, author of *Cocktails: How to Mix Them*, published in 1922. He ought to know. Craddock was his contemporary, and the author of *The Savoy Cocktail Book*, one of the pre-war bibles of mixology.

Appropriately, for a Five Boroughs cocktail, it is very similar to the Bronx, replacing the orange juice with fresh pineapple.

½ slice of fresh pineapple

20 ml (¾ fl oz) red vermouth

20 ml (¾ fl oz) dry vermouth

40 ml (1¼ fl oz) gin

Crush the pineapple with a muddler in the bottom of a cocktail shaker. Fill the shaker with ice, then pour in the two vermouths and the gin. Shake well, then strain into a cocktail glass.

THE GIBSON

There are various stories about the Gibson's origins. Two of them involve characters named Gibson, who would ask bartenders to serve them water in a Martini glass with a silverskin onion garnish so they could tell their drink apart from their friends' alcoholic Martinis. A third version says that the Gibson – a much drier version of the Martini than was fashionable before the Second World War – sported its onion to single it out from its more vermouthified colleagues. **Martinis have become drier and drier over time,** but I think the Gibson's onion makes it a perfect dinner cocktail, *preferably served with a rare grilled steak.*

5 ml (1 tsp) white vermouth

60 ml (2 fl oz) gin

1–3 pearl onions, to garnish

Fill a cocktail shaker with ice and pour in the vermouth. Stir vigorously to coat the ice, then pour in the gin. Stir again. When the cocktail is perishingly cold, strain into a Martini glass and garnish with the onions.

> **KAY'S TIP:** Replace the gin with vodka for a Vodka Gibson.

Parmesan Crisps with
Beef Carpaccio and Rocket

see page 214

THE FINE & DANDY

I think the Fine and Dandy is a bit of a forgotten gem. **It's fresh and sophisticated,** and its pale peach hue is a delight to behold. The thing is, I cannot find out where it came from. So, since every cocktail should have an origin story, here goes mine.

Fine and Dandy was a show written in 1930 by Kay Swift, the first woman to score a full Broadway musical, and a long-time paramour of the legendary George Gershwin. It was a massive hit, and its title number was covered by everyone from Charlie Parker to Barbra Streisand. So I'm going to stick my neck out and say the drink was named for it. On a side note, Kay Swift eloped with a rodeo cowboy in 1939. *She sounds like my kind of girl.*

20 ml (¾ fl oz) fresh lemon juice

20 ml (¾ fl oz) Cointreau

40 ml (1¼ fl oz) gin

a dash of Angostura bitters

Fill a cocktail shaker with ice and add all the ingredients. Shake until icy cold and strain into a Martini glass.

KAY'S TIP: Some people garnish this with a maraschino cherry. I feel it's better without. Either way, sup with Peggy Lee's recording playing in the background.

Pork Crackling with Rosemary and Fennel

see page 216

THE FRENCH 75

Is this a gin cocktail or a Champagne cocktail? I say gin, but either way it's said to have the kick of a French 75mm field gun. This was created by Harry MacElhone of Harry's Bar, New York, in 1915. **It definitely packs a punch – you have been warned!**

40 ml (1¼ fl oz) gin

20 ml (¾ fl oz) fresh lemon juice

10–20 ml (2–4 tsp) sugar syrup (see page 17)

chilled Champagne, to top up

a twist of lemon, to garnish

Fill a cocktail shaker with ice and add the gin, lemon juice and sugar syrup to taste. Shake well, then strain into a Champagne flute. Top up with Champagne and garnish with a twist of lemon.

TOM'S APRIL SOUR

Our friend Tom Williams' fragrant cocktail evokes memories of English spring and early summer with its bright citrus tang and hints of elderflower and cucumber. He designed it specifically to pair with similar notes in the Hendrick's gin, while the egg white gives it a dreamy lemon meringue finish. Sip while sprawled on a cool grass lawn.

50 ml (1¾ fl oz) Hendrick's gin

25 ml (¾ fl oz) fresh lemon juice

25 ml (¾ fl oz) elderflower cordial

a dash of egg white

a thin slice of cucumber, to garnish

Pour the gin, lemon juice, elderflower cordial and egg white into a cocktail shaker and shake until emulsified. Fill the shaker with ice and shake again until it's very cold. Strain into a glass and top with the cucumber float.

THE NEGRONI ▷

This is alleged to have been invented in Florence by Count Negroni, who asked the bartender at the Hotel Baglioni to strengthen his Americano with a spot of gin, but no one knows if this is actually true. Orson Welles was one of the first Americans to write about it, saying 'the bitters are excellent for your liver, the gin is bad for you. They balance each other out'. James Bond orders one in the short story *Risico*. So consider it a drink endorsed by proper drinkers.

20 ml (¾ fl oz) gin

20 ml (¾ fl oz) Campari

20 ml (¾ fl oz) red vermouth

a slice or a twist of orange, to garnish

Pour the gin, Campari and red vermouth over 3–4 ice cubes in a tumbler. Stir the alcohols together until they are very cold. Garnish with a slice or twist of orange, ideally a blood orange.

KAY'S TIP: if you replace the gin with prosecco, you get a *Negroni Sbagliato*, or a Wrong Negroni.

THE GIMLET

I'm sure there's someone out there who calls this a Lime Martini. But we won't go there. **It's one of the classics.** The Savoy in London used to make two versions of this, a Gimlet with equal parts gin and lime, and a Gimblet with two parts gin to one part lime. In the former, the lime was Rose's lime cordial; in the latter, it was fresh juice. My Gimlet blends the two.

50 ml (1¾ fl oz) gin

5 ml (1 tsp) Rose's lime cordial

a twist of lime, to garnish

Fill a cocktail shaker with ice and add the gin and lime cordial. Stir vigorously. Strain into a Martini glass and garnish with a twist of lime.

THE FIZZ & THE COLLINS

The Fizz, the Collins and the Sour are closely related. Each involves a similar blend of lemon juice, sugar and spirit, then the recipes deviate. In essence, a Fizz is a shaken Sour that is topped up with soda. And a Collins is a stirred Sour that is…topped up with soda. Does it make a difference? Generations of bartenders say so. *I suggest that, on a hot summer's night, they are both equally refreshing.*

THE GIN FIZZ

25 ml (¾ fl oz) fresh lemon juice

50 ml (1¾ fl oz) gin

10 ml (2 tsp) sugar syrup (see page 17)

chilled soda water, to top up

Fill a cocktail shaker with ice and pour in the lemon juice, gin and sugar syrup. Shake hard until ice-cold. Strain into an ice-filled highball glass and top up with soda water.

Variations: You can substitute the gin for rye or bourbon, or for Nick Cuthbert's sloe gin (see page 115). You can also replace the lemon juice with Meyer lemon juice, which is slightly sweeter, to make a Meyer Lemon Fizz.

THE TOM COLLINS

I am particularly attached to the Tom Collins, for it was down to this very drink, sipped under a starry Mumbai sky on board the good ship *Oriana*, that yours truly became more than a twinkle in her mother's eye…

25 ml (¾ fl oz) fresh lemon juice

50 ml (1¾ fl oz) gin

10 ml (2 tsp) sugar syrup (see page 17)

chilled soda water, to top up

To garnish:

a slice of lemon

a maraschino cherry

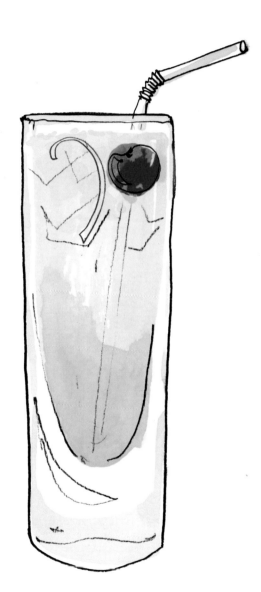

Fill a Collins glass with ice and pour in the lemon juice, gin and sugar syrup. Stir well to combine, then top up with soda water. Garnish with a slice of lemon and a maraschino cherry, and serve.

Variations: If gin makes a Collins into Tom, then other spirits will change its name as well. It won't surprise you to know that no one can agree on these names, so here are a few options:

Vodka	The Joe Collins, Vodka Collins or Comrade Collins
Bourbon	Colonel Collins, and sometimes John Collins
Irish whiskey	Michael Collins (though if you swap the sugar syrup for Grenadine, it becomes a Kevin Collins)
Scotch whisky	Sandy Collins or Jock Collins
Cognac	Pierre Collins
Calvados	Jack Collins, after American Applejack
Tequila	Juan, Pepito, Ruben or José Collins, variously
Pisco	The Pisco Collins, or occasionally Phil Collins, after the singer – can you feel it in the air tonight…?

VODKA
VODKA AND JUICES

How many times have you heard someone at the bar order vodka and orange? They could have asked for a Screwdriver. While they may not seem like cocktails, they're still mixed drinks, and most vodka and juice combinations have a name. And if they don't, you can always make one up. It just makes it all a little more fun. Here are four of my favourites.

THE SEABREEZE

Fill a glass with ice. Pour in 30 ml (1 fl oz) vodka. Top up with cranberry juice.

THE GREYHOUND

Fill a glass with ice. Pour in 30 ml (1 fl oz) vodka. Top up with grapefruit juice.

THE SALTY DOG

Rub the top of a glass with a fresh-cut piece of lime or grapefruit, then rim it with sea salt. Fill the glass with ice. Pour in 30 ml (1 fl oz) vodka. Top up with grapefruit juice.

And, of course, where would we be without the Bloody Mary? I love it so much, I've devoted a whole section to The Bloody Mary Bar (see pages 54–6).

THE SCREWDRIVER

Fill a glass with ice. Pour in 30 ml (1 fl oz) vodka. Top up with orange juice.

THE TUCC' OF CLASS

When it came to naming a cocktail for the delightful actor Stanley Tucci, I knew it had to combine some New York sophistication – it is after all the city at the centre of the world – with a little Italian heritage. **So what could be more sophisticated than a twist on a Negroni?** And what could say heritage better than a classic Italian liqueur?

20 ml (¾ fl oz) vodka

20 ml (¾ fl oz) Cynar

20 ml (¾ fl oz) triple sec

2–4 drops of orange bitters

a slice of orange, to garnish

Fill a tumbler with large cubes of ice. Pour in the vodka, Cynar and triple sec and stir together until they're very cold. Then add the bitters. Garnish with the orange slice and serve. Stylishly.

THE COSMOPOLITAN

There's a misconception about the Cosmopolitan: people assume that, because it's pink, it should be sweet. **Ideally, a good Cosmopolitan should be rather tart with a sweet back.** It was reinvented by the legendary Toby Cecchini, who used to run the equally legendary bar Passerby (one of my favourites), when he worked at The Odeon in New York (another of my favourites) in the late 1980s. If ever a drink conquered a city, this was it. *Honour is due.*

25 ml (¾ fl oz) vodka

25 ml (¾ fl oz) triple sec

20 ml (¾ fl oz) fresh lime juice

a splash of cranberry juice
(just to stain the drink, no more)

a twist of lemon, to garnish

Fill a cocktail shaker with ice. Add the liquid ingredients, and shake like hell. Pour into a chilled Martini glass and garnish with a fat twist of lemon.

THE GLENEAGLES

This is named for Gleneagles, which overlooks Mgarr Harbour on the island of Gozo in the Mediterranean Sea. It's an utterly unpretentious fishermen's bar with nary a cocktail in sight and a view to die for. But if you were to capture the flavours of Calypso's Isle in a drink, I think oranges and local herbs might be a step in the right direction. So how about an infused vodka, some Campari – it is based on a bitter orange, after all – and Aperol. Oh, yes!

40 ml (1¼ fl oz) infused vodka (see below)

10 ml (2 tsp) Campari

10 ml (2 tsp) Aperol

a dash of fresh orange juice

a dash of orange bitters

a twist of lemon, to garnish

Infused vodka:

14 cm (5½ inch) strip of orange peel

1 thyme sprig

7 basil leaves

350 ml (12 fl oz) vodka

To infuse the vodka, remove the peel from the orange carefully, making sure you leave behind as much pith as possible. Then put the peel and the herbs in the bottle of vodka, seal it closed and leave in the fridge or a cool, dark place for 6–12 hours, shaking occasionally. Strain through a tea-strainer into a clean, sterilized bottle.

To make the drink, place all the ingredients in an ice-filled shaker. Seal tightly, then shake vigorously. Strain into a cocktail glass and garnish with the twist of lemon.

THE MOSCOW MULE

Technically, a drink made with a spirit, juice and ginger ale or beer is known as a buck. Perhaps because they do. The Moscow Mule is said to have been invented at the Cock'n'Bull, a British-themed pub on the Sunset Strip in Hollywood, by its owner Jack Morgan some time in the early 1940s. **If you like, you can replace the vodka with bourbon to make a Kentucky Mule.** Both have a kick.

30 ml (1 fl oz) fresh lime juice

60 ml (2 fl oz) vodka

90 ml (3 fl oz) chilled ginger beer

Fill a glass with ice and pour in the lime juice and the vodka. Stir them together, then add the ginger beer.

Note: These were originally served in copper cups – if you can find one, go for it!

◀ THE BLOODY MARY BAR

Sunday mornings are never quite the same without the newspapers, **a long brunch with friends** and an icy, spicy Bloody Mary in hand. Make a classic drink as per the recipe below, then let your guests customize their cocktail by adding something – or everything – from the Bloody Mary Bar!

60 ml (2 fl oz) vodka

celery salt and freshly ground black pepper

½ tsp grated horseradish

Tabasco sauce

Worcestershire sauce

a wedge of lemon

chilled tomato juice, to top up

Fill a highball glass with ice. Pour in the vodka. Season with a good pinch of celery salt and several grinds of black pepper. Then add the horseradish and several dashes of Tabasco and Worcestershire sauce – the more the merrier in my book. Squeeze in the lemon wedge and top up with tomato juice. Stir and serve.

Blood Mary Bar Options
- Pickled chillies on sticks
- Dill pickles, quartered
- Oysters on the half shell
- Sticks of salsify
- Sticks of celery and whole, long carrots
- Cooked prawns on skewers
- Stuffed olives on sticks
- Strips of crispy bacon
- A selection of hot sauces

FRANK PLUNKETT'S BULLSHOT

Marilyn Monroe said of the Bullshot: 'What a terrible thing to do to vodka!' I disagree – they're surprisingly delicious. Dad used to make them on a Sunday, using cold, cold tinned beef consommé. We'd sit on the terrace in Gozo, sipping icy-salty goodness. Apparently, the drink was invented at the Caucus Club in Detroit in the early 1950s. Which would fit in with Dad, who worked for Ford and was often Michigan-bound for work. When he made them, he was a bit of a purist, only going for the vodka, consommé and plenty of black pepper. But **feel free to add any of the optional extras below**.

50 ml (1¾ fl oz) vodka

90 ml (3 fl oz) beef consommé

a pinch of freshly ground black pepper

a squeeze of fresh lemon juice

a few dashes of Worcestershire sauce (optional)

2 dashes of Tabasco (optional)

a pinch of cayenne pepper (optional)

a pinch of celery salt (optional)

Pour the vodka and consommé into a glass and add the seasonings. Stir together thoroughly, then top up the glass with ice. Serve at once. Alternatively, mix all the ingredients in a mug and top up with freshly boiled hot water. It's very warming!

BOURBON, RYE & WHISKY
THE LIFE OF RYE-LEY

A cocktail from the palate of my imagination, and inspired by the resurgence of rye whiskey. I like to think of it as the invention of a rye-swillin' gamblin' man who's hit lucky and, high on the Hogge (excuse me), decides to fancify his drink with **a riff on a Champagne cocktail.** Prosecco seems to work very well here, but if you're really feeling flush, you can also stretch to Champagne.

a sugar cube

a few dashes of Jerry Thomas' Own Decanter bitters

20 ml (¾ fl oz) rye whiskey

chilled prosecco or Champagne, to top up

a maraschino cherry, to garnish

Put the sugar cube in the bottom of a stemmed glass (a coupe would be perfect) and douse it with a few dashes of the bitters. Pour in the rye, then top up with icy cold prosecco. Garnish with the cherry.

Note: If you like it dirty, add a splash of maraschino cherry juice.

Who was Jerry Thomas?
Jerry Thomas, aka The Professor, is the Godfather of Bartending. His 1862 book, *The Bar-Tender's Guide* or *How To Mix Drinks*, was the first book on drink mixing ever written. Like many of the drinks he mixed, we don't know very much about him – his story is murky at best. He was a bartender, a gold prospector and a show producer variously. But each time we go to the bar or mix a drink, we are just a little bit indebted to him.

> **KAY'S TIP:** Jerry Thomas's Own Decanter bitters is made by the Bitter Truth and is readily available online.

THE MINT JULEP

This is the classic cocktail of the American south, and especially of Kentucky. There are variants as you move towards the Gulf. The Georgia version features brandy with a dash of peach brandy to round it out. Pre-Civil War recipes call for Cognac. And I recently had one made with moonshine (white bourbon) and strawberries. So, once you're *au fait*, **feel free to dabble.** Oh, and if you can find a porch with a swing seat to sit on while drinking it, all the better!

a sugar cube

a few mint sprigs

60–80 ml (2–2½ fl oz) bourbon

Place the sugar in the bottom of a glass or cup with 6 or so mint leaves. Crush them together to release the mint oils. Then pack the glass with crushed ice and pour in the bourbon. Stir until the glass is thoroughly frosted. Add more ice and a couple of sprigs of mint, to garnish, and serve.

THE WHISKEY SOUR

You can make a classic Sour with any spirit you like, to the proportions below. **The trick is balancing the lemon and sugar** to achieve the perfect lip-puckering proportions that make this drink truly satisfying – some lemons are sourer than others. I sometimes like to make this with Meyer lemons if I can find them. And when I can't and I'm looking for that flavour, I replace 5–10 ml (1–2 tsp) of the lemon juice with freshly squeezed orange juice to find the proper tang. And speaking of orange, back in the bar in Bang Saray (where I might have been known to belt out a song or two after a couple of these), they used to make them with an equal mix of orange and lime juice, too. *Delicious!*

50 ml (1¾ fl oz) bourbon or blended Scotch whisky

20 ml (¾ fl oz) fresh lemon juice

20 ml (¾ fl oz) sugar syrup (see page 17)

To garnish:

a slice of lemon

a maraschino cherry (optional)

Pour all the ingredients into a cocktail shaker with plenty of ice, and shake until cold. Strain into a Sour glass and serve garnished with a slice of lemon and a maraschino cherry if you like.

Note: You can also serve this on the rocks in a tumbler or Old Fashioned glass.

THE BOSTON SOUR

Some bars serve this version in place of a classic Whiskey Sour, but it is technically a different drink. Using the same ingredients as listed opposite, pour all the liquids into an empty shaker along with **1 small egg white**. Shake well to emulsify. Then add lots of ice and shake again until cold. Strain into a Sour glass and garnish as opposite.

THE MANHATTAN

Some say the Manhattan was invented for a testimonial dinner at the Manhattan Club on 29 December 1874, held in honour of Samuel J Tilden, one of the only US presidential candidates to have won an absolute majority but to have lost in the Electoral College. Others claim it was created for a banquet hosted in New York by Winston Churchill's mother. It's also apparently the national drink of the tiny Frisian island of Föhr, in north-west Germany, where they favour proportions of one part red vermouth to two parts whiskey. It was brought back by deep-sea fishermen who had taken a liking to it on their travels. You see? *You can only learn such curious things in a bar.*

5 ml (1 tsp) red vermouth

a dash of Angostura or Peychaud's bitters (optional)

60 ml (2 fl oz) bourbon or rye whiskey

a maraschino cherry or a twist of lemon, to garnish

Fill a cocktail shaker with ice and add the vermouth and the bitters, if you're using them. Stir vigorously, then add the whiskey. Stir until it's ice-cold. Strain into a Martini glass and garnish with a cherry or a twist of lemon.

Note: I prefer my Manhattan dry, so feel free to add more vermouth if it suits your taste.

For a picture of this drink, see page 36

MANHATTAN

THE BROOKLYN

If ever there was a drink which marks the cocktail's resurgence, it's the Brooklyn. It was forgotten for years, partly because cocktails in general were out of fashion, but mostly, I think, because one of its key ingredients, Amer Picon, can be very hard to find. But as barkeepers and cocktail fans have crawled through old recipe books looking for inspiration, its sheer deliciousness has been rediscovered.

KAY'S TIP: Amer Picon remains difficult to find. The San Francisco-based Torani Company, who are well known for their syrups, makes Torani Amer, which is widely used as a replacement. Its bitter orange and gentian notes make it a very good substitute, and you should be able to find it online.

60 ml (2 fl oz) rye whiskey
20 ml (¾ fl oz) dry vermouth
10 ml (2 tsp) Amer Picon
10 ml (2 tsp) maraschino
a maraschino cherry, to garnish

Fill a cocktail shaker with ice. Add the liquors and stir until very cold. Strain into a cocktail glass and garnish with a maraschino cherry.

Note: Amer Picon is a French liqueur with a distinct flavour of bitter orange. It has been reformulated over the years, so this Brooklyn recipe won't replicate the 1908 original completely, but it's still awfully good.

For a picture of this drink, see page 36

THE GREEN GIMLET

This recipe comes from my friend Michel Dozois, a great barsmith and the founder of Névé Ice – he makes all the ice cubes for *Mad Men*! He thinks this gimlet variation is ideal for the summer. With the lime juice and basil, **it's fresh and straightforward,** not unlike Michel himself.

3–4 basil leaves, plus 1 to garnish

60 ml (2 fl oz) Scotch whisky

30 ml (1 fl oz) fresh lime juice

10 ml (2 tsp) sugar syrup (see page 17)

Put the basil leaves in a shaker, pour in the liquids, then muddle them together. Add ice and shake vigorously until it's very cold. Strain into a tumbler over a large ice cube and serve garnished with a basil leaf.

HYDE & SEEK'S MODERN MAD MEN

This updated Old Fashioned comes from the popular Hyde and Seek, chef and restaurateur Ian Kittichai's modern gastropub, just off the Wireless Road in Bangkok. And it's just as fabulous as it sounds: throw on some 1960s tunes, make some of these and twist the night away!

a sugar cube

3 dashes of celery bitters

50 ml (1¾ fl oz) rosemary-infused bourbon (see below)

10 ml (2 tsp) pear liqueur

a rosemary sprig, to garnish

Rosemary-infused bourbon:

350 ml (12 fl oz) bourbon

5 rosemary sprigs

To make rosemary-infused bourbon, pour the bourbon into a jug and add the rosemary sprigs. Leave for 24 hours, then strain into a clean, sterilized bottle.

Using the same method as you would to make an Old Fashioned, place the sugar in the bottom of a tumbler. Douse it in the bitters and crush them together. Add a large cube of ice and pour in the spirits. Stir the drink together to chill it, and garnish with a sprig of rosemary.

THE SAZERAC

The Sazerac began life **as a kind of Old Fashioned,** made with Sazerac de Forge et Fils Cognac and a local bitters made by Antoine Peychaud, a Creole apothecary who had moved to the French Quarter of New Orleans from the West Indies. It's now the city's signature cocktail. As they say in the Big Easy, *Laissez les bon temps rouler.*

a sugar cube or 5 ml (1 tsp) sugar syrup (see page 17)

a few dashes of Peychaud's bitters

60 ml (2 fl oz) rye whiskey

10 ml (2 tsp) Herbsaint

a piece of lemon peel

Pack a tumbler with crushed ice or place it in the freezer until it's really cold. Put the sugar into a second tumbler, add the bitters and crush them together. Add the rye and stir well. Discard the ice from the first tumbler and pour in the Herbsaint. Swirl it about the glass, then discard. Pour in the rye and bitters. Then twist the lemon peel and smear its oils around the rim of the glass. Add or discard, to taste.

Note: If you can't find Herbsaint, you can substitute another anise-flavoured liquor such as Pernod.

THE OLD FASHIONED

Along with the Swizzle, the Old Fashioned is pretty much ground zero for the cocktail, dating back to at least 1806. And although there are numerous variations on the recipe, the essentials of the drink have hardly changed. All you need is sugar, bitters and hard liquor. And, *as I'm an old-fashioned girl, this is my kind of drink.*

1 sugar cube

several dashes of Angostura bitters

60–80 ml (2–2½ fl oz) bourbon or rye whiskey

To garnish:

a twist or a wedge of orange

a maraschino cherry (optional)

Place the sugar cube in the bottom of a tumbler and saturate it with a few dashes of Angostura bitters, to taste. Crush the sugar and the bitters together with a muddler – some people like to add a dash of water at this point to help the sugar dissolve. Then add a few large cubes of ice. Pour in the bourbon or rye and stir briefly to amalgamate. Garnish with the orange and a maraschino cherry if you like.

Note: One of the best Old Fashioneds I have had was made with baconized bourbon. To make it, buy the smokiest cure of streaky bacon you can find – hickory smoked is best – and cook up enough for a good bacon sandwich. While it's cooking, pour 350 ml (12 fl oz) bourbon into a clean jam jar. When the bacon's done, make your sandwich – you can't let it go to waste – then pour the bacon fat into the jar with the bourbon. You should have a good 2–3 tbsp. Leave to steep for a day, then put the jar into the freezer until the bacon fat has completely solidified. Strain through a coffee filter paper into a clean, sterilized bottle. The bourbon should now look like, well, bourbon, but it will have a distinct smoky bacon aroma. Delicious!

THE PIMLICO

This mash-up of a Julep and a Daiquiri was created by chef-proprietor David Lentz at his fabulous Hollywood restaurant, The Hungry Cat. David says that it's named after the Pimlico Race Course in Baltimore, where Seabiscuit won one of his most famous races. **It's perfect for summer drinking,** al fresco, ideally with a seafood spread just like the ones you would find at David's restaurant. (If you go there, make sure to check out their fantastic wine list, too. I think it's one of the best curated lists in Hollywood.)

2 mint sprigs

30 ml (1 fl oz) sugar syrup (see page 17)

45 ml (1½ fl oz) bourbon

2 tbsp fresh orange juice

4 tsp fresh lime juice

Remove the leaves from 1 mint sprig and muddle them in a cocktail shaker with the syrup. Fill the shaker with ice. Pour in the bourbon, orange juice and lime juice. Shake well. Strain over ice into a tumbler and garnish with the remaining mint sprig.

THE MASSA(MAN)HATTAN

From Kin Shop, a modern Thai restaurant in New York City, comes this sultry, Siamese-influenced Manhattan, invented by their former manager Julia Travis. It's a cool cocktail warmed with southern Thai curry spices, a perfect union of East and West. *I'm just kicking myself that I didn't think of it first!*

60 ml (2 fl oz) rye whiskey (at Kin Shop they use Old Overholt)

20 ml (¾ fl oz) sweet red vermouth

20 ml (¾ fl oz) Massaman syrup (see below)

a twist of orange, to garnish

Massaman syrup:

1 tbsp mace

5 cinnamon sticks

2 tbsp coriander seeds

3 cardamom pods

15 cloves

½ nutmeg, broken into pieces

1 litre (1¾ pints) water

800 g (1 lb 10 oz) dark soft brown sugar

To make the syrup, place all the spices in a dry frying pan over a medium heat and stir often until fragrant and lightly toasted. Add the water and bring to the boil. Add the sugar, bring it back to the boil and immediately remove from the heat. At Kin Shop, they cool the syrup quickly in an ice bath, but you can leave it uncovered in the fridge until it's cool. Strain the syrup into a sterilized jar. It will keep in a cool place for up to a month.

To make the drink, fill a shaker with ice and pour in the ingredients. Shake vigorously, then strain into a chilled cocktail glass. Garnish with the orange twist.

TEQUILA & MEZCAL
THE BANDERITA

Sangrita: should it have tomato in it? Some say yes, some say no. I can't decide.
I'm not The Arbitrator. So here's The Banderita, featuring **a sangrita with tomato.**

a shot of tequila

a shot of fresh lime juice

50 ml (1¾ fl oz) fresh orange juice

50 ml (1¾ fl oz) fresh tomato juice

**a few slugs of the Mexican
hot sauce of your choice**

a pinch of salt

Line up three shot glasses and fill 1 with tequila and 1 with lime juice.
Mix the remaining ingredients in the third glass to make up the colours
of the Mexican flag. Down them in that order or, frankly, any way you
like. Exclaim loudly in a *Woo-hoo!* or *Venga!* sort of a way. Go again.

And here's one without tomato: a shot of Tequila with a sangrita chaser.

a shot of tequila

50 ml (1¾ fl oz) fresh orange juice, chilled

50 ml (1¾ fl oz) fresh grapefruit juice, chilled

a good squeeze of fresh lime juice

a few slugs of the Mexican hot sauce of your choice

a pinch of salt

First fill a shot glass with the tequila. Then pour all the other ingredients into a tumbler and stir well. Serve together.

THE MARGARITA

When I lived in Los Angeles, the Margarita was my drink of choice – you could say it was **one of my Five-a-Day.** I was a terror: I used to go to the Formosa Cafe at about half past one in the morning, steal the keys as the owner, Vince, was locking up, and force him to make me one. I'd always order another, so in the end he served them to me in a pint glass so he could clean down without interruption – something that has proved a solid basis for a life-long friendship.

As to the drink itself, it was either created by Carlos Orozco at Hussong's Cantina in Ensenada, in Baja California, in 1941 and named for the daughter of the German ambassador OR it was invented by bartender Santos Cruz at the Balinese Room in Galveston, Texas, in 1948 and named for Peggy Lee (Peggy being short for Margaret, hence Margarita).

It's a great party drink and perfect at the end of a (Baja) California summer's day.

a wedge of lime

salt

30 ml (1 fl oz) fresh lime juice

30 ml (1 fl oz) Cointreau or other triple sec

60 ml (2 fl oz) white tequila

Wipe the lime wedge around the rim of a tumbler, then dip the rim in salt to coat it. Fill a cocktail shaker with ice and add the lime juice, triple sec and tequila. Shake rhythmically to Peggy Lee's *Fever* until very cold. Fill the tumbler with fresh ice, then strain the drink over the top. Squeeze in the wedge of lime, add it to the drink, and serve.

Note: To make a Frozen Margarita, place the tequila, lime juice and triple sec in a blender with plenty of ice. Blitz until smooth, then serve in a salt-rimmed glass.

THE TEQUILA SUNRISE

I'll bet that, when (or if) you think of the Tequila Sunrise, you picture a tall drink of layered colours, reds through oranges, reminiscent of…well…a sunrise. You'd be right. And therein hangs a tale. That familiar cocktail was preceded by an earlier, very different beast, said to have been invented by bartender Gene Sulit at the Arizona Biltmore Hotel, which opened in those heady pre-Crash days of early 1929. Sulit's drink fell out of fashion. But then, in the early 1970s, Billy Rice and Bobby Lozoff at the Trident Restaurant in Sausalito took up the name to make a new drink. In a 2012 interview with writer and bartender Jeff Burkhart, **Lozoff says he mixed one for Mick Jagger in 1972, who introduced it to the Rolling Stones,** and it was then spread across the USA. And in 1973, the Eagles also named a song for it, and thus it conquered the world. *Very rock 'n' roll, man!* These are my takes on both of them.

THE ARIZONA BILTMORE VERSION

40 ml (1¼ fl oz) tequila

20 ml (¾ fl oz) crème de cassis

a squeeze of lime

chilled soda water, to top up

3 slices of lime, to garnish

Fill a glass with cracked ice. Add the tequila, then the crème de cassis and a squeeze of lime. Top up with soda and garnish with the lime slices.

THE ROLLING STONES VERSION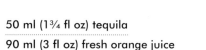

50 ml (1¾ fl oz) tequila

90 ml (3 fl oz) fresh orange juice

10 ml (2 tsp) grenadine

To garnish:

a slice of orange and/or a maraschino cherry

Fill a glass with ice. Pour in the tequila, then the orange juice, and then add the grenadine. Do not stir. The grenadine will sink to the bottom of the glass. Garnish and serve.

BUN BANG FAI

The Bun Bang Fai (meaning Rocket Festival) is one of the signature drinks at Soul Food Mahanakorn in Bangkok. It was created by its owner, Jarrett Wrisley, and his bartender Markus Bernthaler, to be spicy, sour and good with grilled Thai food. *I'd serve this with Thai Fishcakes* (see page 167).

2 tiny pieces of bird's eye chilli

60 ml (2 fl oz) white tequila

40 ml (1¼ fl oz) fresh lime juice

30 ml (1 fl oz) Monin Orgeat almond syrup

a dash of egg white

Muddle the chili in the bottom of a shaker. Add all the liquid ingredients, including the egg white, and shake vigorously to emulsify. Now add some ice and shake again for about 15 seconds, until it's really cold. Strain into an ice-filled tumbler and serve.

Note: Choose tequila made from 100 per cent agave if possible.

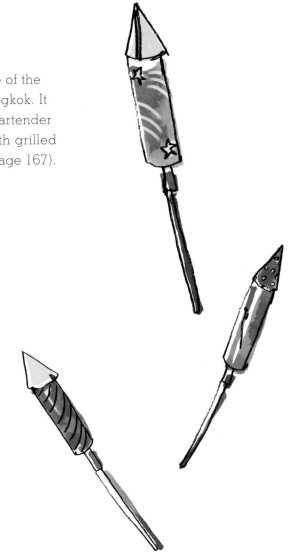

THE DEL RIO

Even before I went to work in the fashion business, Dolores Del Rio was one of my heroes. Effortlessly chic, achingly beautiful, she was also whip smart and fiercely proud of where she came from. She was the first Mexican movie star, with a hugely successful career in Hollywood silents and talkies before the war, and a leading figure in the golden age of Mexican cinema, too. So, in naming a drink for her, I wanted something that reflected her roots in the State of Durango, and which **captured a hint of her elegance and integrity.** So the mezcal and the bitters fly the flag for Mexico, the orange of the Curaçao provides some citrus warmth, and the peach speaks both as a fruit of Durango and a Renaissance symbol for the heart. And the gardenia? Miss Del Rio always swore that eating gardenia blossoms maintained her flawless complexion.

2 ripe flat peaches

40 ml (1¼ fl oz) mezcal reposado

20 ml (¾ fl oz) Pierre Ferrand Dry Curaçao or Grand Marnier

a couple of dashes of Bitter Truth Xocolatl Mole bitters

gardenia petals, to garnish

Squeeze the peaches by hand over a clean bowl to release their juice, making sure you retain all the pulp and skin in your hand. Then fill a cocktail shaker with ice and add 20 ml (¾ fl oz) of the peach juice with all the remaining liquid ingredients. Stir until icy cold. Strain into a stemmed glass, and garnish with the gardenia petals.

LUCA MISSAGLIA'S ON THE WAY TO SARONNO

Luca Missaglia is the bar manager at the Hart Brothers' Quo Vadis in London's Soho. **He is effortlessly smooth and charming as only an Italian can be.** In creating this drink, Luca wanted to reflect the story behind amaretto, how a young, beautiful widow and the painter Bernardino Luini came to fall in love while he painted her as the Madonna in a fresco, and how her gift to him was apricot kernels steeped in brandy. *Thus amaretto was born.* We just know we like it…and we can indeed be On Our Way to Saronno any time you like.

3 dashes of Cynar

30 ml (1 fl oz) passion fruit purée (see below)

30 ml (1 fl oz) tequila reposado

45 ml (1½ fl oz) Disaronno amaretto

Passion fruit purée:

3–4 passion fruits

5 ml (1 tsp) sugar syrup (see page 17)

To garnish:

a mint sprig

½ passion fruit

freshly ground black pepper

To make the passion fruit purée, cut the passion fruits in half and scoop out the seeds and pulp into a sieve set over a non-metallic bowl. Press through the sieve with a spoon, leaving the seeds behind. Add a little sugar syrup just to take the sharpness off it. You will need about 5 ml (1 tsp) sugar syrup per 50 ml (2 fl oz) passion fruit purée (about 3 passion fruits' worth).

Fill a glass with crushed ice and pour in all the liquid ingredients, including the passion fruit purée. Swizzle it to mix and top up with more crushed ice, if necessary. Garnish with the mint, passion fruit half and a twist of black pepper.

Note: You can buy passion fruit purée by the kilo. It's easy to find online, but I'd only recommend it if you plan to make a lot of these, because it's quite easy to purée your own.

GARRA DE TIGRE (THE TIGER'S CLAW)

Guelaguetza is one of my favourite Mexican restaurants in Los Angeles, specializing in Oaxacan regional food and famous for its *moles*. Opened by Fernando Lopez in 1994, it's now run by his children Bricia and Fernando. And this cocktail is one of the stars at the bar, invented by Fernando Snr to show off mezcal's mixing potential when he was a *mezcalero*. Enjoy!

a wedge of lime

½ tsp chilli salt (see below)

60 ml (2 fl oz) fresh lime juice

30 ml (1 fl oz) sugar syrup (see page 17)

60 ml (2 fl oz) mezcal

Rub the lime wedge around the rim of a glass, then dip it in the chilli salt to coat it. Put the lime juice, syrup and mezcal in a blender with a cup of ice and blitz until it's smooth and frothy. Pour into the glass and serve.

Note: At Guelaguetza, their chilli salt is actually gusano salt from Oaxaca. It's made with ground-up maguey worms which you find in mezcal. To make a substitute chilli salt, mix 1 part chilli powder to 3 parts salt.

Ceviche Shots
see page 199

RUM
THE CLASSIC RUM PUNCH

"One of sour

Two of sweet

Three of strong

Four of weak."

This is a cocktail with its very own poem. Stir it up,
put some Jamaican mento on the stereo and kick back.

20 ml (¾ fl oz) fresh lime juice

40 ml (1¼ fl oz) sugar syrup (see page 17)

60 ml (2 fl oz) rum, preferably Appleton V/X

a slice of orange, to garnish

Stir together the lime juice, sugar syrup and rum
in a large glass, then top up with cracked ice.
Stir again and garnish with a slice of orange.

**Jerk Chicken and Fresh
Mango Salsa Poppadums**

see page 219

THE ZOMBIE

The next time you find yourself in Los Angeles, head east (it will almost certainly be east) along Sunset, towards Los Feliz and Silverlake. Shortly after you pass the Vista cinema, you will almost certainly miss the Tiki-Ti, founded by Ray Buhen in 1961, and now run by his son Mike. **Here you can taste a Zombie that's as close to the original as you can find.**

The Zombie was created at Don The Beachcomber bar in 1934 – probably not by Don, though he always said it was. Don's 'special' drinks, of which the Zombie was one, were always made out of sight, behind the bar, by a crew known as The Four Boys. Ray was one of the boys. Realizing he'd never make any tips in the back room, Ray struck out on his own, taking the secret recipes with him. This is not his recipe, which remains a closely guarded secret, but it's as near as I can get!

60 ml (2 fl oz) white rum

30 ml (1 fl oz) dark rum

30 ml (1 fl oz) fresh orange juice

30 ml (1 fl oz) fresh pineapple juice

30ml (1 fl oz) passion fruit purée (see page 86)

15ml (½ fl oz) Bacardi 151 rum

To garnish:

a maraschino cherry

¼ slice of orange

a chunk of pineapple

Fill a cocktail shaker with ice and pour in all the ingredients apart from the 151 rum. Stir the ingredients together, then strain into an ice-filled Collins glass. Float the 151 rum over the top and garnish with the fruit, skewered on a long cocktail stick.

THE FORMOSA'S MAI TAI

No one's exactly sure how the Formosa Cafe in Hollywood became famous for Mai Tais. It's not a Tiki bar, after all. But its owner Vince Jung says there are two stories. The drink was either **requested by Elvis, a Formosa regular who once tipped a waitress with a brand new Cadillac** – he'd come to like them after shooting his Hawaii films. Or it was the drink of choice for the props guys from the movie version of *South Pacific*. Both left signed photos. Go visit, prop up the bar and decide for yourself.

50 ml (1¾ fl oz) white rum

20 ml (¾ fl oz) amaretto

50 ml (1¾ fl oz) fresh orange juice

50 ml (1¾ fl oz) fresh pineapple juice

30 ml (1 fl oz) dark rum

To garnish:

a maraschino cherry (optional)

a piece of pineapple (optional)

a cocktail umbrella (optional)

Fill a shaker with ice. Add the white rum, amaretto and the juices. Shake it. Hard. Perhaps to the rhythm of *Rock-a-hula Baby* or *There's Nothing Like a Dame*. Strain into a glass over ice, then float the dark rum over the top. Garnish with the fruit and an umbrella if you like.

Note: The Formosa's use of amaretto is where it differs from the original, which contained orgeat syrup to provide the almond flavour, and orange Curaçao to provide an extra hit of alcohol.

THE (BOAC) RUM SWIZZLE

The Rum Swizzle is one of the oldest rum punches on record, dating back to the 1700s and one of the national drinks of Bermuda. I first discovered the recipe printed on the side of a tropically decorated wooden BOAC cocktail cup from the early '60s. Back in the day, a stewardess in First Class *had* to know 12 cocktails by heart for the in-flight bar service. The BOAC version cuts back on the juices. And since it *really* comes from Bermuda, the rum MUST be Goslings.

50 ml (1¾ fl oz) dark rum

25 ml (¾ fl oz) light rum

25 ml (¾ fl oz) fresh lime juice

25 ml (¾ fl oz) fresh pineapple juice

25 ml (¾ fl oz) fresh orange juice

10 ml (2 tsp) grenadine

To garnish:

a slice of orange

a maraschino cherry

Fill a shaker with crushed ice. Add all the ingredients, then shake hard until it goes frothy. Strain into a highball glass and garnish with a slice of orange and a maraschino cherry.

Note: This was originally made with a syrup known as falernum, which comes from Barbados and is flavoured with almond, ginger, cloves and allspice. If you prefer, try to track some down or infuse a homemade sugar syrup (see page 17) with the spices, then add a little almond essence to finish it.

THE MOJITO

Ah...the Mojito! **It's become wildly fashionable of late.** Many bartenders I know hate to make it because it takes time to mix well. But at home there's no rush, which makes it ideal. And it dates from the days when rum was so rough you had to do something, anything, to make it taste better.

I know the Mojito is Cuban and I should really make this with Havana Club, but if you can find it, try using the white Domaine de Séverin rhum agricole from Guadaloupe. *It adds real depth to the drink.*

2 mint sprigs

a sugar cube

30 ml (1 fl oz) fresh lime juice

60 ml (2 fl oz) white rum

chilled soda water, to top up

Strip the leaves from 1 of the sprigs of mint and put them in a glass with the sugar cube. Crush them together with a muddler to release the oils. Add the lime juice and stir together. If you're not in a hurry (for which, read, gasping for a drink) let it macerate for a couple of minutes while you make a snack.

Fill the glass with crushed or cracked ice. Add the rum, stir again, and top up with soda water. Garnish with the remaining sprig of mint and serve.

THE SEAWIND

This drink is designed to be long, strong and astringent – **the perfect antidote to too many overly sweet tropical drinks.** I think it's best enjoyed at sunset, preferably on a beach (though a back garden with a gazebo will do), in preparation for a spicy-spicy dinner.

40 ml (1¼ fl oz) white overproof rum

30 ml (1 fl oz) fresh lime juice

several good dashes of Angostura bitters

20 ml (¾ fl oz) sugar syrup (see page 17)

chilled soda water, to top up

a slice of lime, to garnish

In a highball glass, stir together the overproof, lime juice, bitters and sugar syrup. Fill the glass with ice, then top up with soda water. Garnish with a slice of lime.

THE RUM RANCH ▶

This is a drink about dreams or, rather, our crazy dream to build a ranch to distil rum in California. The crazy part being that California's not exactly known for its sugar production. *The dream part being that it would be rather lovely.*

a sliver of medium to hot red chilli

60 ml (2 fl oz) aged rum, preferably 7-year-old Havana Club

10 ml (2 tsp) sugar syrup (see page 17)

10 ml (2 tsp) fresh orange juice

10 ml (2 tsp) fresh lemon juice

a dash of pimento bitters

a twist of lemon, to garnish

First muddle the chilli in the bottom of a cocktail shaker. Then fill it with ice and add all the rest of the ingredients. Shake hard until icy cold and strain into a cocktail glass. Garnish with a twist of lemon.

Note: When I came up with this, I planned to use Meyer lemon juice. If you can find a Meyer lemon, you'll need 20 ml (¾ fl oz) of its juice to replace the orange and lemon juices in the recipe.

The Avocado Project
see page 104

The Classic Daiquiri
see page 105

THE AVOCADO PROJECT

Julian Cox is one of LA's top bartenders and responsible for the drinks at two of my favourite restaurants, Rivera and Picca Peru. He created this drink for Picca. I think **it's already a modern classic,** and something to try when you're feeling adventurous. As with all of Julian's recipes, he is very specific about the type of liquor to use. So if you can't find Banks 5 Island rum, use 12-year-old Appleton or Havana Club. But it won't be quite the same.

60 ml (2 fl oz) Banks 5 Island Rum

30 ml (1 fl oz) fresh lime juice

1½ tsp raw agave nectar

2 heaped tbsp sweetened avocado purée (see below)

Sweetened avocado purée:

1 ripe avocado

3 tbsp raw agave nectar

¼ tsp lemon juice

To garnish:

a piece of lime peel

sea salt

To make the sweetened avocado purée, mash the flesh from the avocado with the raw agave nectar, then pass it through a fine sieve. Add the lemon juice and mix well.

Fill a cocktail shaker with ice and add all the ingredients. Shake long and hard, then strain into a stemmed glass. Twist the piece of lime peel over the drink to release the aromatics, then serve garnished with a small pinch of salt.

For a picture of this drink, see page 102

THE CLASSIC DAIQUIRI

A Classic Daiquiri is simple beyond measure. It's one of the oldest Cuban cocktails, dating from the late 1800s, and is guaranteed to make a party go with a swing. It was also **a favourite of Ernest Hemingway,** a very particular drinker, who even had his own Daiquiri variation created for him by the bartender at the El Floridita in Havana. I think that its very simplicity takes the Daiquiri close to perfection. It's a proper drink for grown-ups, so you can take your strawberries and your bananas and make a fruit salad. *This is the real thing.*

50 ml (1¾ fl oz) white rum, preferably 3-year-old Havana Club

20 ml (¾ fl oz) fresh lime juice

10 ml (2 tsp) sugar syrup (see page 17)

a slice of lime, to garnish

Fill a cocktail shaker with crushed ice. Add all the ingredients, then shake hard until it goes frothy. Strain into a cocktail glass and garnish with a slice of lime.

Note: If you'd like a Frozen Daiquiri (I wouldn't, personally), put all the ingredients in a blender with a cupful of ice and blitz until smooth.

For a picture of this drink, see page 102

HOT BUTTERED RUM

There's nothing more warming or more soothing than a mug of hot buttered rum. It's a drink as old as...well... it's not quite as old as time, **but it's been drunk by pirates and presidents,** and bounders and bishops for centuries. *This drink is as resolutely unfashionable as a Christmas jumper, but just as welcome at the right moment!*

30 g (1¼ oz) spiced butter (see below)

60 ml (2 fl oz) aged or dark rum

freshly boiled water, to top up

freshly grated nutmeg, to garnish

Spiced butter:

200 g (7 oz) dark soft brown sugar

125 g (5 oz) unsalted butter, softened

¾ tsp freshly grated nutmeg

1½ tsp ground allspice

2 pinches of ground mace

a pinch of ground cinnamon

a pinch of salt

To make the spiced butter, put all the ingredients in a mixing bowl and stir together. Turn out on to a sheet of clingfilm (plastic wrap) and wrap tightly. The spiced butter will keep in the fridge for up to 1 month, or you can freeze it. It makes enough for 8–10 drinks.

To make the drink, put the butter in a mug and add the rum. Top up with freshly boiled water and stir until the butter has melted and emulsified into the drink. Garnish with a grating of fresh nutmeg.

KAY'S TIP: There is a quicker version. Dissolve 1 tsp sugar in a little boiling water in a mug. Add a good slug of rum and 30 g (1¼ oz) butter. Top up with more hot water and grate some nutmeg over the top. Job done.

MRS. BROWNE'S EGGNOG

This comes from a handwritten recipe book belonging to Granny Alice, my husband's Jamaican great-grandmother. I've had to adapt it slightly to update it, but it's serious, potent, rich and, well, glorious.

SERVES 6–8

2–3 tbsp sugar syrup (see page 17)

1 egg

125 ml (4 fl oz) Cognac

65 ml (2¼ fl oz) rum, preferably Appleton's

chilled whole milk, to top up

freshly grated nutmeg, to garnish

KAY'S TIP: Granny Alice says that, to make a hot version, one simply replaces the ice with boiling water.

Pour the sugar syrup into a cocktail shaker, add the egg and the spirits and shake until the ingredients are well emulsified. Pour into a pint glass.

Put 4–5 ice cubes in a blender and blitz until they have the texture of snow. If a couple of the cubes are still solid, don't worry. Scoop the ice into the pint glass and top up with milk. Return everything to the blender and blitz again to mix thoroughly.

Pour out into eggnog or punch cups, holding back the foam but making sure everyone gets some. Garnish with freshly grated nutmeg.

BANG SARAY
BOUNCE

¾ OZ. LIME JUICE
¾ OZ. PINEAPPLE JUICE
1 OZ. DARK RUM
2 OZ. LIGHT RUM
½ OZ APRICOT LIQUEUR
SHAKE WITH CRACKED ICE
& DECORATE WITH FRUIT SLICE

THE BANG SARAY BOUNCE

This was invented by my mum, Betty, when we lived in the picturesque Thai fishing village of Bang Saray. It was an homage to evenings in the piano bar, telling tall tales of the day's catch. *It's sunny, bright and sharp – just like her.*

30 ml (1 fl oz) dark rum

60 ml (2 fl oz) light rum

20 ml (¾ fl oz) fresh lime juice

20 ml (¾ fl oz) fresh pineapple juice

15 ml (½ fl oz) apricot liqueur

a slice of lime, to garnish

Fill a shaker with ice, add the rums, juices and the liqueur. Shake until very cold. Strain into a glass and garnish with a slice of lime.

THE STATEN ISLAND

Curiously, there is no agreed recipe for a Staten Island cocktail, which may be one of the reasons why some people often call it 'the forgotten borough'. Researching this book, I've found drinks which claim the name that are made with coffee vodka or with Jack Daniels and energy drinks, but there's nothing that fits in with the other Borough Cocktails. So it's time to roll up my sleeves and invent one. It's inspired by the Palmetto (aged rum and red vermouth, with orange bitters and a twist), which is in turn based on a Manhattan. So it seems rather appropriate to take the concept back and to name it as it should have been named in the first place.

15 ml (½ fl oz) Cocchi Vermouth di Torino

60 ml (2 fl oz) Pampero Aniversario rum

a good dash of lemon bitters

To garnish:

a flamed twist of lemon (see right)

a maraschino cherry

Fill a cocktail shaker with ice and add the vermouth, rum and lemon bitters. Stir vigorously until it's cold. Pour out into a stemmed glass, garnish with a maraschino cherry and, finally, flame a twist of lemon over the top.

KAY'S TIP: To flame a twist, cut a strip of peel from the fruit, then ignite a match or a lighter and squeeze the twist into the flame over the drink. You will ignite and caramelize the oils in the peel, and add a little spectacle to making the drink.

For a picture of this drink, see page 36

WINE, BEER & OTHER SPIRITS
KHUN SOMPONG'S THAIJITO

Khun Sompong Boonsri was the head barman at the Mandarin Oriental, Bangkok's Bamboo Bar for over 30 years. It is one of Bangkok's classic watering holes, lubricating the great and the good (and the louche) since 1953. I've propped up its bar on rather too many occasions, alternating my order between my beloved Martini and this, **Khun Sompong's elegant variation on a Mojito.** (The Bamboo Bar is very proud of the fact that not one, but two former James Bonds really rather like it. I'll tell you which if you ask me nicely.)

2 tsp brown sugar

1 lemon grass stalk, tough outer leaves removed, core thickly sliced

½ lime, cut into quarters

2 x 1 cm (¾ x ½ inch) piece of fresh root ginger, peeled and finely shredded

30 ml (1 fl oz) Mekhong Thai whisky

chilled soda water, to top up

a piece of sugar cane, peeled, or a lemon grass stalk, to garnish

Put the sugar, lemon grass, lime and a good pinch of ginger strips into a shaker and muddle them together well. Pour in the Mekhong and stir. Fill the shaker with ice and shake vigorously. Strain into an ice-filled tumbler or Old Fashioned glass and top up with soda water. Garnish with a lemon grass stalk or, like Khun Sompong, with a stick of freshly peeled sugar cane, and serve with a straw if you like.

Note: Mekhong is often called a whisky. It's not. It's more akin to a rum made with cane sugar and rice. Officially, it's labelled as a Thai spirit. If you can't find it, take your pick of whisky or rum!

SANGRIA

The idea of flavouring wine goes back to the Romans. And since they, allegedly, took vines to Spain, it seems apt that Spain is where this flavoured wine originates. Almost every bar or restaurant has its own version. In southern Spain, they make a variation called *zurra*, which uses peaches – so feel free to play around with different fruits and different sweetnesses to make the drink your own.

SERVES 6–8

750 ml (1¼ pints) red wine

2 lemons, cut into wedges

1 orange, cut into wedges

2–3 tbsp caster sugar

30 ml (1 fl oz) Grand Marnier or aged orange Curaçao

75 ml (2½ fl oz) Spanish brandy

500 ml (17 fl oz) chilled soda water

Mix the wine, fruit, sugar, Grand Marnier or curaçao and brandy together in a jug. Cover and leave to steep for at least an hour, but no more than 6. When you're ready to serve, add the soda water and pour into ice-filled glasses.

Potato, Manchego and Saffron Tortilla
see page 189

CHILCANO DE PISCO

Pisco is the national drink of Peru, an *aguardente* made with grapes in both Peru and Chile. **It's potent stuff.**

60 ml (2 fl oz) pisco

a dash of Angostura bitters

1 tablespoon fresh lime juice, preferably key lime

125 ml (4 fl oz) chilled ginger ale

lime slices, to garnish

a wedge of lime, to serve

Fill a glass with ice, then add the pisco, the bitters and the lime juice. Stir briefly, then add the ginger ale. Garnish with a couple of thin slices of lime, and serve with an extra wedge of lime on the side.

NICK CUTHBERT'S SLOE GIN FIZZ

Sloes are at their best for picking after the first frost. But Nick says why wait? Just put them in the freezer for a day, then thaw them out before making sloe gin.

For the sloe gin:

500 g (1 lb) sloes, frozen then defrosted

750 ml (1¼ pints) gin

300 g (10 oz) sugar

Mix everything together in a large jar or screw-top bottle, and leave for 1–3 months in a cool dark place. Make sure you give the bottle a good shake every day. When it's done, strain it into a sterilized bottle. It will keep indefinitely.

For the Sloe Gin Fizz:

20 ml (¾ fl oz) sloe gin (see above)

100 ml (3½ fl oz) chilled prosecco or English sparkling wine

Pour the sloe gin into a glass and top up with prosecco or English sparkling wine.

THE CLASSIC CHAMPAGNE COCKTAIL

Known by some, back in the day, as Chorus Girls' Milk, **the Champagne Cocktail is one of the oldest going.** Recipes date back deep into the 1800s. This version, though, probably emerged some time in the early 1890s, but no one is entirely sure.

The brandy, ideally Cognac, is optional, and its quantity is a matter of taste. In *The Big Sleep*, General Sternwood preferred it to make up one-third of the drink. In *Casablanca*, neither Victor Lazlo nor Captain Renault seem to care. ***So it's really up to you.***

1 sugar cube

a few dashes of Angostura or Peychaud's bitters

Cognac, to cover the sugar cube

chilled Champagne, to top up

a twist of orange, to garnish

Put the sugar in the bottom of a flute and douse it with 3–4 dashes of bitters. Pour in enough Cognac to cover the sugar. Then top up carefully with Champagne, remembering that the bitters will make the Champagne fizz more than usual. Finally, squeeze the oils from a piece of orange peel over the surface of the drink. Then add the twist and serve.

Note: If you have time (or freezer space), chill the glass before you make the drink.

Quails' Eggs with Celery Salt, Cumin and Black Pepper

see page 188

THE CAIPIRINHA

While rum is distilled from molasses, cachaça is distilled from the cane juice itself. It is an *aguardente*, and unique to Brazil. Hardly surprising, then, that **the Caipirinha is the Brazilian national cocktail!** No one knows quite where it came from. Some say it began life as a cold remedy, made with honey and garlic in addition to the usual ingredients.

1 lime, cut into 8 wedges

1–2 sugar cubes

60 ml (2 fl oz) cachaça

Put the lime wedges and sugar in a glass and muddle them together well. Pour in the cachaça and top up with ice. Stir, and serve.

Note: In Brazil, people say the best Caipirinhas are made with *limões galegos* or key limes. So, if you can find them, why not give it a go?

Payon's Peanuts
see page 179

THE AMERICANO

This is a sharp drink. Long and not too strong, **with a delicious tang of bitterness,** it's the perfect start to a long night when you feel the need to pace yourself. Of course, your order may be confused with a cup of coffee, something which seems to be happening in bars FAR TOO OFTEN, I'm afraid to say.

30 ml (1 fl oz) Campari
30 ml (1 fl oz) red vermouth
chilled soda water, to top up
a slice or a twist of orange,
to garnish

Fill a glass with ice. Pour in the Campari and vermouth and stir them together. Top up with soda water and garnish with a slice of orange or a twist of peel.

THE SPRITZ

This is THE Venetian drink of choice. Cool, bittersweet and colourful – perfect when watching the world go by in St Mark's Square...or wherever you live! Traditionally it is made with white wine and sparkling water, but I like this version with prosecco.

15 ml (½ fl oz) Campari or Aperol

125 ml (4 fl oz) chilled prosecco, or equal parts white wine and fizzy water

1 orange chunk, preferably blood orange

1 green olive in brine, rinsed

Pour the Campari or Aperol into a glass. Top up to about half way with the prosecco or wine and water. Pop in a cube of ice. Skewer the orange chunk and the olive on a long cocktail stick and place in the glass. Serve with the bowl of ice on the side, and a heavy dose of insouciance!

THE SOMERSET LEVELLER

I blame this drink on my husband. Fred was terribly excited by the idea of this book and immediately offered to help. And this is it. 'Somerset' for the Somerset cider brandy, and 'Leveller' because Somerset has Levels (a couple of these will certainly level you) and, he says, the Levellers were rural rebels in the English Civil War. *Power to the people.*

5 ml (1 tsp) crème de mûre

60 ml (2 fl oz) Somerset cider brandy

a rosemary sprig

1.5 cm (¾ inch) cube of green apple, soaked in fresh lime juice

a dash of lemon bitters

Fill a cocktail shaker with ice. Add the crème de mûre and the cider brandy, and stir until it's very cold. Strain into a stemmed glass. Strip the leaves from the rosemary sprig, leaving a nice tuft at the tip, and impale the apple cube upon it. Place this in the drink. Add a dash of lemon bitters, and serve.

THE SIDECAR

One of the few classic *and* good Cognac cocktails (there's the Corpse Reviver out there, too, among others, but it has crème de menthe in it – who were they kidding?), it's thought that the Sidecar was invented during the First World War. **The Ritz in Paris claims it as their own.** Harry (of Harry's Bar in Paris) MacElhone's 1922 book, *Harry's ABC of Mixing Cocktails*, attributes it to Pat MacGarry, bartender at the Buck's Club in London. He should know!

20 ml (¾ fl oz) fresh lemon juice

20 ml (¾ fl oz) Cointreau or triple sec

40 ml (1¼ fl oz) Cognac

a twist of orange, to garnish

Fill a cocktail shaker with ice and pour in the lemon juice, triple sec and brandy. Shake until icy cold, then strain into a cocktail glass. Garnish with a twist of orange.

THE MICHELADA

This Mexican *cerveza preparada* is mightily refreshing on a hot day. It exists in many different versions, so feel free to experiment with different combinations of sauces and spices to make the drink your own.

1–2 limes, halved

sea salt

several dashes of Worcestershire sauce

several dashes of Tabasco or other hot sauce

several dashes of soy sauce or Maggi sauce

freshly ground black pepper

20 ml (¾ fl oz) tomato juice or Clamato juice (optional)

chilled beer, to top up

First rim the glass with salt: wipe a piece of lime around the rim, then dip the rim in sea salt to coat. Fill the glass with ice, then squeeze in all the lime juice. Add the sauces, a few grinds of pepper and the tomato juice, if you're using it. Stir the juice and sauces together, then top up with cold beer.

Note: I don't like a lot of tomato, because I think it tastes like beery gazpacho. If it's your thing, add as much as you like! Clamato juice is a mixture of tomato juice, spices and clam broth, sold mainly for use in cocktails.

THE HIX FIX

Invented at Mark Hix's Oyster and Fish House in Lyme Regis, **I think this is a perfect English drink.** It's very simple. It makes the best of a local ingredient – in this case, Julian Temperley's riff on a maraschino cherry, enhanced with his own apple eau de vie. And it brightens a day at the seaside, which heaven knows we need in England. It also sets you up perfectly for a feast. *Job done.*

1 morello cherry in Somerset eau de vie

125 ml (4 fl oz) chilled Nyetimber sparkling wine or Champagne

Place a cherry with 1–2 tsp of the liqueur in the bottom of a Champagne coupe. Add the sparkling wine or Champagne. Serve at once.

KAY'S TIP: You can buy the Hix Fix cherries from Mark's restaurants or online.

THE GLOOM CHASER

Zesty, springy and bright, this does indeed chase the blues away. It was originally designed to help you over your hangover, but I think it's just as good as an aperitif after a long day.

20 ml (¾ fl oz) Grand Marnier

20 ml (¾ fl oz) orange Curaçao

20 ml (¾ fl oz) fresh lemon juice

a splash of grenadine

a twist of lemon or lime,
to garnish

Fill a shaker with ice, pour in the liquid ingredients, and shake until very cold. Strain into a cocktail glass and garnish with a twist of lemon or lime. Or both.

THE BELLINI

From Harry's Bar in Venice, the Bellini is an early summer pleasure. Some people make this with Champagne, some people use nectarines. They are wrong. It must be made with peaches and prosecco. Accept no substitutes.

2 tbsp freshly pulped peaches, preferably white ones

chilled prosecco, to top up

Spoon the peach pulp into the bottom of a glass and top up carefully with prosecco. I say carefully, because the peach will make it fizz up even more than usual, something which has often caught me out! Stir briefly to lift the peach into the drink, and serve.

Arancini
see page 184

Cheddar-Parmesan Biscuits
see page 181

Non-alcoholic Drinks

It goes without saying that sobriety is a good thing, especially if you're driving. And I see no reason why those who aren't on the sauce shouldn't have a delicious drink too.

NON-ALCOHOLIC DRINKS
THREE LEMONADES

On a hot summer's day, there's nothing more refreshing than a cold glass of lemonade. So here are three of them – I call that refreshment [ice] cubed!

1 CLASSIC LEMONADE

SERVES 8–10

175 g (6 oz) caster (superfine) sugar

225 ml (8 fl oz) water

350 ml (12 fl oz) fresh lemon juice (about 6–8 lemons)

1 litre (1¾ pints) chilled water

Place the sugar and water in a saucepan over a medium heat and stir until the sugar has completely dissolved. Do not allow to boil. Pour it into a heatproof measuring jug and allow to cool.

Pour half of the syrup into a jug. Add the lemon juice and water and taste the lemonade, adding more of the syrup if it is too sharp for your taste. Serve over ice in highball glasses.

2 BASIL & MINT LEMONADE

SERVES 8–10

1 quantity Classic Lemonade (see left)

20 g (¾ oz) basil leaves

20 g (¾ oz) mint leaves

Pour the Classic Lemonade into a blender, then tear in the basil and mint leaves. Blend until almost smooth, then strain through a fine sieve into a jug. Serve over ice in highball glasses.

Note: The simple syrup here is not as sweet as the one on page 17. This is a matter of taste, and to balance out the refreshing sour-sweet zing of a lemonade. If you'd like to add more sugar, it's entirely up to you.

3 RASPBERRY LEMONADE

SERVES 10

300 g (10 oz) raspberries

175 g (6 oz) caster (superfine) sugar

225 ml (8 fl oz) water

350 ml (12 fl oz) fresh lemon juice (about 6–8 lemons)

1 litre (1¾ pints) chilled water

Rub the raspberries through a sieve using a wooden spoon, then discard the pips. Follow the method for Classic Lemonade (see far left) to make a sugar syrup. When the syrup has cooled, mix it with the raspberry purée and the lemon juice, then top up with the chilled water. Serve over ice in highball glasses.

THE RUDE BOI

I came up with this for my nephews Alex and Alastair when they were younger. Originally we used Lilt, a pineapple-flavoured fizzy drink, instead of ginger beer because they loved it. If anything, it makes the drink sweeter than it is already!

60 ml (2 fl oz) shop-bought mango and passion fruit smoothie

30 ml (1 fl oz) sugar syrup (see page 17)

chilled ginger beer, to top up

a slice of orange or a maraschino cherry, to garnish

Fill a Collins glass with ice. Pour in the smoothie and the sugar syrup and top up with chilled ginger beer. Stir together, garnish with a slice of orange or a cherry and serve at once.

THE SHIRLEY TEMPLE

This was allegedly invented in the late 1930s for the child star at Chasen's, Beverly Hills. Or the Brown Derby. Or the Royal Hawaiian. (They were all in on the act!) *She has said, apparently, she never liked it much.*

chilled ginger ale or 7 Up, or an
equal mix of both

a dash of grenadine

a maraschino cherry, to garnish

Fill a glass with ice cubes and pour in the sodas. Add a dash of grenadine and garnish with a maraschino cherry.

3

4

Rosemary and Chilli
Roasted Walnuts
see page 179

FOUR REFRESHING DRINKS

Sharp, bright and reviving, these will perk up even the most jaded palate.

1 THE CUMFETANYA

In Mexico, they call hibiscus *flor de jamaica*. So to make this variation on a hibiscus *agua fresca* all the more Jamaican, I've added some allspice and ginger, and named it for my husband's grandparents' house in Montego Bay (it means 'we will stay here to the end'). It's red and round, fresh and aromatic, and perfect for a sunny day. **Note that you need to make this the day before you want to serve it.**

SERVES 8–10

15 g (½ oz) dried hibiscus flowers or roselle

1 tbsp dried allspice berries, crushed

2 cm (¾ inch) piece of fresh root ginger, peeled and roughly chopped

250 ml (8 fl oz) water

75 g (3 oz) caster (superfine) sugar

1 litre (1¾ pints) chilled water

lime wedges, to serve

Place the hibiscus flowers, allspice and ginger in a saucepan with the water and bring to the boil. Bubble hard for 5 minutes, then remove from the heat and add the sugar. Stir to dissolve, then pour everything into a heatproof jug and top up with the chilled water. Leave to macerate overnight, then strain and serve in tall glasses over ice, squeezing a wedge of fresh lime over each serving to finish the drink.

For a picture of this drink,
see page 136

2 LIME & LEMON GRASS SPRITZER

Fizzy, lime-y, fragrant, this is **the epitome of the word refreshing.**
Add some mint or basil sprigs to garnish, if you like.

SERVES 2

1 lemon grass stalk, tough outer leaves removed,
core sliced, plus an extra stalk to garnish

60 ml (2 fl oz) fresh lime juice

30 ml (1 fl oz) sugar syrup (see page 17)

chilled soda water, to top up

Divide the sliced lemon grass between 2 Collins glasses and muddle to release the oils. Fill the glasses with ice and pour in the lime juice and the sugar syrup. Top up with soda water, stir briefly and garnish with the remaining lemon grass stalk.

For a picture of this drink,
see page 136

3 THE TAMARIND COOLER

Khun Jao Fa is the executive assistant manager at the charming Tamarind Village Hotel in Chiang Mai. He's also a fantastic cook. He came up with this very refreshing alcohol-free drink for the hotel's bar menu, and I think it's an absolute winner. I love the way the sour tamarind cuts through the sweetness of the guava and pineapple. It slips down very easily on a hot, sticky day.

90 ml (3 fl oz) pink guava juice

90 ml (3 fl oz) tamarind juice (see below)

90 ml (3 fl oz) fresh pineapple juice

15 ml (½ fl oz) grenadine syrup

15 ml (½ fl oz) sugar syrup (see page 17)

15 ml (½ fl oz) fresh lime juice

Tamarind juice:

1 tbsp pure tamarind concentrate

100 ml (3½ fl oz) water

To garnish:

a slice of lime

a maraschino cherry

For a picture of this drink, see page 137

To make the tamarind juice, mix the pure tamarind concentrate with the water.

Fill a cocktail shaker with ice and pour in all of the liquids. Shake very well until it's very cold. Strain into a highball glass, garnish with the slice of lime and a maraschino cherry and serve.

Notes:

You can find pure tamarind concentrate in most Asian supermarkets.

If you don't live in a citrus-growing area, limes often aren't as punchy as they could be. You may find, once you've mixed this, that you want to add another squeeze of lime juice, just to make the drink come together.

Sometimes it can be hard to find pure guava juice. A 'guava juice drink' can be used instead, but leave out the sugar syrup to compensate.

4 PROPER ICED TEA

Please, please, please don't use any strangely flavoured teas for this: it's a straight-up, straight-backed proper iced tea recipe, designed to refresh you on a super hot day. This cold-brew method gives you a beautiful clear tea. And, whatever you do, don't stint on the ice.

SERVES 4

4 tea bags or 4 tsp loose-leaf tea

1 litre (1¾ pints) cold water

lemon wedges, to garnish

Place the tea in a jug and add the water. Leave it to infuse in the fridge, stirring occasionally, until it reaches a delicious mahogany colour – about 2–4 hours, depending on how strong you like your tea. Strain the tea if necessary and set aside until you're ready to serve. Fill 4 Collins glasses with ice and divide the tea between them. Garnish with lemon wedges and serve.

KAY'S TIP: If I want to sweeten my iced tea, I prefer to use agave nectar instead of sugar.

For a picture of this drink, see page 137

LEVAN-THAI-NE ICED COFFEE

I love the spiced coffees you find all over the Levant, and I love the Thai-style iced coffee, sweetened with condensed milk. So I thought I'd combine the two. I like to imagine this being drunk by Lebanese traders after they've inspected their cargo on the banks of the Chao Phraya river!

SERVES 4

12 cardamom pods

1 star anise

2 cm (¾ inch) piece of cinnamon stick

3–4 tbsp ground coffee

sugar, to taste

Use a pestle and mortar to bash the spices to release their flavour. Mix them with the ground coffee, place them in the coffee section of a 9-cup (550 ml/18½ fl oz) moka pot, fill the bottom with water and brew. When it's done, pour out the coffee and leave to cool.

To serve, divide the cold coffee between 4 ice-filled tea glasses. Add sugar to taste.

KAY'S TIP: To serve white, mix the coffee with condensed milk until it reaches the colour you desire. Then pour the mixture into ice-filled tea glasses. The condensed milk should sweeten it sufficiently.

The Food

The canapés in this section are delicious, and I have tried to ensure there's a mixture of quickly whip-up-able snacks alongside things that take a little bit of effort.

PLATTERS, NUTS & THINGS ON STICKS
THREE SOUP SHOTS

The great thing about these savoury cocktails is that you can make them well ahead of time. You may want to serve these with little spoons.

1 TOMATO AND BASIL SOUP WITH GRILLED CHEESE SANDWICHES

Before I say anything else, I will plead with you to make this soup only when you can get ripe, lush tomatoes: it will make such a difference to the taste and the colour. The little grilled cheese sandwiches on the side are a winner every time!

MAKES 24–28

500 g (1 lb) tomatoes

1 tbsp olive oil

½ onion, chopped

2 garlic cloves, chopped

750 ml (1¼ pints) vegetable stock

1–2 tbsp tomato purée (in case your tomatoes are not the best)

a large handful of basil, torn

sea salt and freshly ground black pepper

little grilled cheese sandwiches, to garnish (see below)

Grilled cheese sandwiches:

a little butter

8 slices white bread

enough sliced cheese for 4 rounds of sandwiches

KAY'S TIP: Make sure you don't serve the soup shots too hot: people may burn themselves by knocking it back and it will be hard to hold. Also make sure you have heatproof glasses!

Plunge the tomatoes into a bowl of boiling water, leave for 1–2 minutes, then drain and slip off their skins. Deseed the tomatoes and chop them roughly. Heat the olive oil in a large saucepan over a low heat. Add the onion and sweat gently until soft. Add the garlic and cook for a minute or 2 more. Add the tomatoes and stir well, then add the stock and tomato purée and bring to the boil.

Reduce the heat and simmer for 5–10 minutes, then season with salt and pepper. Remove from the heat and allow the soup to cool for a few minutes. Transfer to a blender or food processor and blend until smooth. Add the basil and blend again until smooth. Taste and adjust the seasoning if necessary. Remove from the heat and set aside.

To make the grilled cheese sandwiches, butter the slices of white bread and make into 4 rounds of sandwiches filled with the sliced cheese, buttered sides out. Cook in a hot, dry frying pan until golden on both sides, then cut into mini-sandwiches and serve with the soup, on sticks if you like. Serve the soup warm or cold, with the little grilled cheese sandwiches on the side.

For a picture of this recipe, see page 146

2 ROASTED BEETROOT, APPLE AND HORSERADISH SOUP

The brilliant **Schiaparelli pink** of this soup is reason enough to make it – it also tastes sublime.

SERVES 24–30

500 g (1 lb) beetroot, chopped into even chunks

250 g (8 oz) Cox's apples, quartered and cored

3 thyme sprigs

1 rosemary sprig

4 tbsp olive oil

1 onion, finely chopped

1 garlic clove, chopped

1 litre (1¾ pints) vegetable stock

2 tsp grated horseradish

a pinch of sugar

sea salt and freshly ground black pepper

sour cream, to garnish (optional)

For a picture of this recipe, see page 147

Preheat the oven to 200°C/350°F/Gas Mark 6. Place the beetroot and apples in a roasting tin with the thyme and rosemary. Drizzle with half the olive oil and season with a little salt and pepper, then cover with foil. Bake for 40 minutes, until the beetroots are soft. Set aside, still covered, to cool. This will help them retain their moisture and make them easier to peel. Peel the cooled beetroot and apples and set aside.

Heat the remaining olive oil in a large saucepan over a medium heat. Add the onion and cook until soft and lightly golden. Add the garlic and stir for another minute or so. Add the beetroot and apples and stir well. Pour in the vegetable stock and bring to the boil.

Simmer for 5–10 minutes, then add the horseradish and sugar and season with salt and pepper. Remove from the heat and allow the soup to cool for a few minutes. Transfer to a blender or food processor and blend until smooth. Taste and adjust the seasoning if necessary.

Serve warm or cold, garnished with a tiny swirl of sour cream, if you like.

3 GREEN GAZPACHO WITH SERRANO HAM CRISPS

Bright green and fresh as a summer's day, this soup should be *served icy cold in small shot glasses.*

SERVES 24–28

300 g (10 oz) cucumber, peeled and roughly chopped

1 green pepper, cored, deseeded and roughly chopped

2 garlic cloves, chopped

4 spring onions, roughly chopped

100 g (3½ oz) baby spinach

125 g (4 oz) frozen peas

a good handful of mint leaves

a good handful of basil leaves

25 g (1 oz) blanched almonds

2 slices of white bread, toasted and roughly torn

juice of ½ lemon

1 tbsp sherry vinegar

sea salt and freshly ground black pepper

4–6 slices of Serrano ham, fried until crisp, to garnish

Pop 5–6 ice cubes into a blender or food processor and blend to crush them. Then add all the remaining ingredients, in batches if necessary, and blend until smooth. Season with salt and pepper. Make sure the soup isn't TOO thick – you want guests to be able to sip it easily – so add a dash of cold water to loosen, if necessary.

Break each of the ham slices into 4 or 6 pieces. Pour the soup into shot glasses and garnish each with a shard of crisp Serrano ham.

For a picture of this recipe, see page 147

THINGS ON STICKS

Everyone loves food on sticks, wrapped in bacon or not. Frankly, I think half the fun of planning a party is the chance to create some **new combinations** and serve some **old classics** (honey-glazed sausage, anyone?).Here are a few of my current favourite things on sticks. They are fairly free form – each idea is for one stick – *just make as many as you need.*

1 FETA, WATERMELON AND MINT

1 cube of good Greek feta cheese

1 cube of ripe watermelon

1 mint leaf

2 ROASTED VEGETABLE MEDLEY

1 roasted slice of baby aubergine (eggplant)

2 roasted slices of carrot

1 roasted slice of courgette (zucchini)

1 piece of roasted red pepper

...all drizzled with some reduced balsamic vinegar

For a picture of these recipes, see pages 152–3

3 FIG, BOCCONCINI, HAM AND BASIL

¼ ripe fig

1 small bocconcini or cube of mozzarella

1 basil leaf

1 strip of prosciutto ham

4 SMOKY THE DUCK

¼ pickled walnut

1 small slice of smoked duck

5 CONQUISTADOR ON HORSEBACK

1 slice of bottled piquillo pepper

1 small slice of Serrano ham

1 cube of Manchego cheese

6 MOO MUAN SUKHOTHAI

These tasty little pork balls are fried crisp and served with a healthy dollop of Sriracha sauce on the side. They're the perfect snack and, of course, perfect on a stick. (A view of Sukhothai's ancient ruins is of course optional, but highly recommended!)

MAKES 18–24

½ tbsp white peppercorns

2 coriander roots

2 garlic cloves, peeled

a pinch of salt

250 g (8 oz) minced pork

1 tbsp Thai fish sauce (nam pla)

3–4 tbsp vegetable oil

1 tbsp rice flour

Sriracha sauce, to serve

Use a pestle and mortar to pound the peppercorns, coriander roots, garlic and salt to a paste.

Place the pork in a bowl and mix in the paste with your hands – really squish it about to get it evenly distributed. Add the fish sauce and mix well again. Heat a little oil in a small pan and fry a tiny piece of the mixture until cooked through. Taste to check the seasoning, adjusting if necessary.

Lightly wet your hands, roll the pork into 18–24 balls and sprinkle them with the rice flour.

Heat a wok or frying pan over a medium heat and, when hot, add the oil, swirling it about a bit. When it is hot again, add the pork balls in small batches and fry for about 2 minutes, or until deep brown on the outside and cooked through.

Drain on kitchen paper for a few moments, then transfer to a plate and put a small bowl of Sriracha sauce on the side. Devour!

TRIO OF TACOS

These make for a **more substantial canapé** or a **light, casual meal** – so you could choose to make one topping or go for all three. For each recipe you will need six corn tortillas, 10 cm (4 inches) in diameter (see my tip below). And remember not to overload them, or the topping will drop all over the carpet! Of course, you could always lay everything out and let people assemble their own.

These are terrific with a long, cooling Michelada (see page 125) or a spiky Margarita (see page 78). Put on some mariachi music and *dream of long, Mexican evenings*...

KAY'S TIP: Tortillas are often larger than 10 cm (4 inches). If so, trim them to size using a very sharp knife and a saucer to cut round. Keep the trimmings – you can fry them in a little vegetable oil until crisp and golden and serve them sprinkled with sea salt. That said, The Cool Chile Company (www.coolchile.co.uk) sell brilliant canapé-perfect 10 cm (4 inch) corn tortillas.

1 CHICKEN AND AVOCADO TACOS

250 g (8 oz) boneless, skinless chicken thighs, cut into small chunks

1 chipotle chilli in adobo sauce, finely chopped

a large pinch of dried Mexican oregano

juice of ½ lime

juice of ½ orange

1 garlic clove, finely chopped

1 tbsp chopped fresh coriander (cilantro)

½ red onion, finely diced

1 tbsp vegetable oil

6 x 10 cm (4 inch) corn tortillas

½ large avocado, peeled and mashed with a little salt and lime juice

sea salt and freshly ground black pepper

lime wedges, to serve

Place the chicken pieces in a large bowl with the chipotle chilli, oregano, lime juice, orange juice, garlic and a good grinding of black pepper. Leave to marinate for 10–15 minutes.

Mix together the coriander (cilantro) and red onion and set aside.

Heat the oil in a frying pan over a medium heat until hot. Season the chicken with a little sea salt and add to the pan with its marinade. Cook, stirring and turning occasionally, until cooked through and golden. Set aside to keep warm.

Heat the tortillas in a dry frying pan over a low heat, turning them once or twice until thoroughly warmed through. Smear a teaspoonful of the mashed avocado on each tortilla. Divide the chicken between them, top with the coriander and onion mixture and serve with wedges of lime on the side.

For a picture of this recipe,
see page 156

2 FISH TACOS WITH SPICY PINEAPPLE SALSA

250 g (8 oz) boneless, skinless firm white fish (monkfish, haddock or tilapia), cut into chunks

1 garlic clove, finely chopped

1 tsp ancho chilli powder

1 tsp ground cumin

a large pinch of dried Mexican oregano

1 tbsp lime juice

1 tbsp vegetable oil

6 x 10 cm (4 inch) corn tortillas

sea salt

lime wedges, to serve

Salsa:

100 g (3½ oz) peeled pineapple, finely diced

½ red onion, finely diced

juice of ½ lime

¼ red habanero or serrano chilli, deseeded and diced (optional)

1 tbsp chopped fresh coriander (cilantro)

Place the fish in a bowl with the garlic, chilli powder, cumin, oregano and lime juice. Mix gently to coat the fish and set aside for 10–15 minutes.

To make the salsa, mix all the ingredients together in a bowl, season with salt and set aside until you are ready to serve.

Heat the oil in a frying pan over a medium heat until hot. Remove the fish from its marinade, season with a little sea salt and add to the pan. Cook, stirring and turning occasionally, until cooked through and golden. Set aside and keep warm. Pour the excess marinade into the pan and let bubble for a couple of minutes to make a sauce.

Meanwhile, heat the tortillas in a dry frying pan over a low heat, turning them once or twice until thoroughly warmed through. Divide the fish and its sauce between the tortillas, top with the salsa and serve with wedges of lime on the side.

For a picture of this recipe, see page 157

3 BLACK BEAN AND AVOCADO TACOS WITH TOMATO SALSA

400 g (14 oz) can black beans

a pinch of dried Mexican oregano

½ tsp ground cumin

6 x 10 cm (4 inch) corn tortillas

½ large avocado, cut into 12 slices

sea salt and freshly ground black pepper

Tomato salsa:

100 g (3½ oz) tomatoes, diced

1 tbsp chopped fresh coriander (cilantro)

½ red onion, finely chopped

½ jalapeño chilli, deseeded and chopped

juice of ¼ lime

To make the salsa, mix all the ingredients together in a bowl, season with salt and set aside.

Place the black beans with their liquid, the oregano and the cumin in a saucepan over a medium heat and season with salt and pepper. Bring to the boil and simmer for a few minutes until the mixture has thickened up. Remove from the heat and roughly mash the beans, leaving some texture, then set aside and keep warm.

Heat the tortillas in a dry frying pan over a low heat, turning them once or twice until thoroughly warmed through. Top each tortilla with a scoop of black beans, 2 slices of avocado and a little tomato salsa.

KAY'S TIP: If you want to serve the tortillas and toppings separately, allowing people to assemble their own tacos, keep the tortillas warm by wrapping them first in some foil and then a decorative cloth, or put them in a tortilla basket.

For a picture of this recipe,
see page 157

ASIAN PLATTER

This selection of Asian-inspired snacks gives you **a little taste of the East.** It is by no means set in stone, so mix and match to your heart's delight – replace one of the dishes with the Sticky Spiced Chicken Wings on page 218, the Moo Muan Sukhothai on page 155, or the Mini Laarp Lettuce Rolls on page 211. Or throw in a curve ball and add another of your favourites. *Don't forget – this is supposed to be FUN!*

1 QUICK CURRY PUFFS

This is not a traditional recipe for curry puffs – crispy pastry parcels full of mild curried chicken and potato – but it works beautifully and takes the hassle out of making fiddly pastry and deep-frying it. The results? A lighter, brighter snack.

MAKES 36–45

2 coriander roots

2 garlic cloves, peeled

2 tbsp vegetable oil

3 tbsp light soy sauce

3 tbsp water

2 tbsp sugar

1 heaped tbsp curry powder

1 onion, finely chopped

200 g (7 oz) boneless, skinless chicken thighs, finely chopped or coarsely minced

200 g (7 oz) potato, boiled and chopped

1 tbsp chopped fresh coriander (cilantro)

3 sheets of ready-rolled puff pastry

1 egg, beaten

sea salt and freshly ground white pepper

For a picture of this recipe,
see page 162

Use a pestle and mortar to grind the coriander roots, garlic and a pinch of salt to a smooth paste. Heat the oil in a wok or frying pan until hot, add the paste and cook, stirring all the time, until it's very fragrant – only a few seconds. Add the soy sauce, water, sugar and curry powder and cook for another minute.

Add the onion, chicken and potato and simmer for a few minutes, stirring now and then, until the chicken is cooked through, adding a splash of water if it's looking a bit dry. Taste and add more salt if necessary – it should be sweet, a little spicy and salty and a little moist. Set aside to cool, then add the chopped coriander (cilantro) and a good few grinds of white pepper.

Preheat the oven to 200°C/400°F/Gas Mark 6. Using a pastry cutter or a template, cut out 36–45 little rounds from the pastry, about 7–8 cm (2¾– 3¼ inches) in diameter. Place a teaspoonful of the chicken mixture on each round, wet the edges of the pastry and fold over to make half-moon shaped parcels, beading the edges of the pastry as you go or using the tines of a fork to seal each parcel decoratively – they will taste delicious either way!

Arrange the parcels on a baking sheet lined with baking paper and brush all over with the beaten egg. Bake for 20–25 minutes or until golden brown and puffed up. Serve warm or at room temperature. You can also make the curry puffs in advance and reheat them: just preheat the oven to 180°C/350°F/Gas Mark 4 and bake for 8–10 minutes, until crisp and hot through.

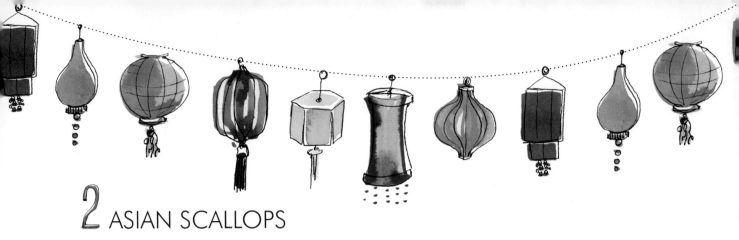

2 ASIAN SCALLOPS

Delicate, yet full of glorious spiky flavours, and served in small ramekins or bowls with the requisite cocktail fork, this is a pretty **simple yet sophisticated canapé.** I wouldn't recommend doing this for a large party as you need to get the scallops out hot and quick.

MAKES 12 PORTIONS

12 large scallops

2 tbsp vegetable oil

4 tbsp soy sauce

a pinch of sugar

3 tbsp rice wine vinegar

2 tsp toasted sesame oil

4 cm (1½ inch) piece of fresh root ginger, peeled and finely slivered

a handful of fresh coriander (cilantro), torn

½ bird's eye chilli, deseeded and chopped (optional)

sea salt and freshly ground black pepper

Pat the scallops dry with kitchen paper and season lightly with salt and pepper. Heat the vegetable oil in a nonstick frying pan over a medium heat until very hot. Add the scallops and sear for about 1–1½ minutes on each side, until just cooked. If they are large, you may need to slice them in half horizontally or cook them a little longer, but be careful not to overcook them.

Remove from the heat and place the scallops in 12 little bowls or china spoons.

Return the pan to the heat and add the soy sauce, sugar, vinegar, sesame oil and ginger. Bubble in the pan for about 30 seconds, then pour a little of the warm dressing over each scallop. Garnish with a scattering of coriander (cilantro) and the chilli, if using. Serve immediately.

For a picture of these recipes, see page 162

3 THAI FISHCAKES WITH CUCUMBER PICKLE

Tiny, tasty fishcakes served with a sweet-sour dipping sauce. *Serve on sticks or with cocktail forks.* Or, if you want to be authentically Thai, in a little plastic bag.

MAKES 16–18

250 g (8 oz) boneless, skinless white fish

2 heaped tbsp Thai red curry paste

1 egg

1 tbsp finely sliced green beans

1 tbsp finely sliced Kaffir lime leaves

1–2 tbsp Thai fish sauce (nam pla)

1 tsp sugar

a pinch of salt

oil, for deep-frying

deep-fried Thai sweet basil leaves, to garnish (optional)

Dipping sauce:

75 ml (3 fl oz) rice wine vinegar

75 g (3 oz) sugar

4 cm (1½ inch) piece of cucumber, quartered lengthways, then sliced

2–3 Thai shallots or 1 shallot, thinly sliced

1 tbsp crushed unsalted peanuts (optional)

1 mild red chilli, sliced (optional)

a pinch of salt

Place the fish, curry paste and egg into a blender or food processor and blend to make a smooth paste. Transfer to a bowl and stir in the beans and lime leaves, then add 1 tbsp of Thai fish sauce, the sugar and salt.

Heat a little oil in a small pan and fry a tiny piece of the mixture until cooked through. Taste to check the seasoning and add more fish sauce or sugar if necessary. Now slap the mixture around the bowl a bit to aerate it – you are aiming for slightly puffy, springy fishcakes.

Make the dipping sauce by heating the vinegar and sugar in a small pan over a low heat until the sugar has dissolved. Let it bubble to thicken it slightly, then remove from the heat and set aside to cool. Add the cucumber, shallot and a splash of cold water to the cooled vinegar with the peanuts and chilli, if using. Season with salt and set aside.

When you are ready to serve, heat the oil for deep-frying until very hot. Wet your hands slightly and shape the fish mixture into 16–18 flattish patties. Fry the fishcakes a few at a time until puffy and golden. Drain on kitchen paper and serve immediately with the dipping sauce, garnished with some deep-fried Thai basil leaves.

4 VIETNAMESE SUMMER ROLLS

A twist on a Vietnamese classic, these can be made up to 3 hours in advance (keep them tightly wrapped in clingfilm/ plastic wrap). You will need to work quickly to wrap the rolls, so have all your ingredients ready. Be sure to have a few spare rice paper wrappers – you know you will tear some!

MAKES 16 ROLLS

16 x 16 cm (6¼ inch) rice paper wrappers

16 large cooked peeled prawns, halved lengthways

125 g (4 oz) carrots, peeled and cut into matchsticks

½ large cucumber, peeled and cut into matchsticks

4 spring onions, sliced very finely lengthways

50 g (2 oz) bean sprouts

50 g (2 oz) rice vermicelli, cooked and drained

1 Baby Gem lettuce, finely shredded

16 mint leaves

16 Thai basil leaves

Thai Peanut Brittle Dipping Sauce (see opposite), to serve

Fill a wide, shallow bowl with hand-hot water. Immerse one rice paper wrapper in the water and leave for about 15 seconds to soften – you want it soft but not sticky or completely dissolved. Lay it flat on a chopping board and place 2 prawn halves just above the centre, flat sides facing up.

Arrange a few pieces each of carrot, cucumber, spring onion and bean sprout in a line across the wrapper, just below the prawns. Top with a small pile of rice noodles and a few shreds of lettuce. Finally, place a mint leaf and a Thai basil leaf on top of that.

Take the bottom of the wrapper and roll it carefully upwards over the filling, then tuck the sides in and roll again to seal. You want the seam to be at the bottom and the prawns to be face up at the top.

Repeat with the remaining ingredients to make 16 rolls, trying to roll them as tightly as possible to avoid spillage. It may take one or two goes to get it right, but don't worry – they will be fine! Cover with a damp tea towel as you go to stop the rolls drying out. And leave a gap between each one or they will stick together.

When you're ready to serve, cut each roll in half on the bias and serve with Thai peanut brittle dipping sauce on the side.

5 THAI PEANUT BRITTLE DIPPING SAUCE

Khun Jao Fa (he of the Tamarind Cooler on page 140) introduced me to this fabulous dipping sauce. I've cut back on the chilli and added some fresh coriander (cilantro) to soften and brighten it a little – but beware! It is still **a spicy little dip.**

3 coriander roots, cut into chunks

3–4 garlic cloves, peeled

2–4 bird's eye chillies

85 g (3¼ oz) peanut brittle, broken into pieces

2 tbsp Thai fish sauce (nam pla)

2 tbsp lime juice

1 tsp sugar

2 tbsp warm water

1 tbsp chopped fresh coriander (cilantro)

Use a pestle and mortar to bash and grind the coriander root, garlic and chilli to a smooth paste. Add the peanut brittle and grind to a coarse mixture, mixing the brittle with the other ingredients as you go.

Add the fish sauce, lime juice, sugar and water, and stir them into the sauce. Finally, stir in the chopped coriander (cilantro). If the sauce is too thick, add a little more water. Transfer to a small bowl and serve with the Vietnamese summer rolls (see opposite).

Note: If you would like to tone down the spice even further, deseed the chillies before you pound them into the paste.

For a picture of these recipes, see page 163

THREE BRUSCHETTE

The sheer simplicity of bruschette – basically, **toast with lovely toppings** – belies their utter deliciousness. But it all comes down to the quality of the bread and its mate…so here I've suggested three toppings. Ideally, the bread should be toasted on a hot griddle, although I'll use the toaster if I'm in a hurry.

For a picture of these recipes, see pages 170–1

1 ROQUEFORT AND MARMALADE ONION BRUSCHETTA

Yes, marmalade onions, NOT the usual onion marmalade. It's quick, easy and absolutely delicious.

15 g (½ oz) unsalted butter

1 tbsp olive oil

2 onions, halved and sliced

2 tbsp good marmalade

a good pinch of marjoram leaves (optional)

6 slices of sourdough bread

150–200 g (5–7 oz) Roquefort cheese

sea salt and freshly ground black pepper

Heat the butter and olive oil in a saucepan over a low heat until melted and hot. Add the onions and cook slowly for about 20 minutes until they are soft and melting but still retain texture. You may want to turn up the heat at the end to get some colour, but make sure they don't burn.

Add a pinch of salt and a good grinding of pepper. Then take the onions off the heat and immediately stir in the marmalade until well combined. Add the marjoram leaves, if using, and stir again. Taste and adjust the seasoning if necessary. Leave to cool, then store in the refrigerator until ready to serve.

Toast the bread slices and cut in half. Smear with a liberal amount of Roquefort, then top with some marmalade onions and serve.

2 RICOTTA, POMEGRANATE AND THYME BRUSCHETTA

Bright **ruby jewels** on a snowy ricotta backdrop…

6 slices of sourdough bread

1 garlic clove, halved

200–250 g (7–8 oz) ricotta di butala

100 g (3½ oz) pomegranate seeds

a small handful of thyme leaves

sea salt and freshly ground black pepper

Toast the bread and rub it with garlic while it's still warm. Cut the slices in half and smear with the ricotta. Sprinkle with pomegranate seeds and thyme leaves, season with salt and pepper and serve.

> **KAY'S TIP:** Choose very good-quality sourdough bread to make bruschetta. You could use baguettes instead, in which case, each recipe is enough to top 18 slices.

3 LARDO AND ROSEMARY BRUSCHETTA

The fatty, unctuous lardo, the spiky rosemary and the crunch of sea salt. *Perfection.*

MAKES 12

6 slices of sourdough bread

1 garlic clove, halved

good extra virgin olive oil, for drizzling

12–18 very thin slices of lardo

a handful of rosemary leaves, finely chopped

sea salt and freshly ground black pepper

Toast the bread and rub it with garlic while it's still warm. Drizzle with a little extra virgin olive oil and cut each slice in half.

Drape a slice of lardo over each bruschetta and top with a pinch of rosemary, a grind of pepper and a pinch of sea salt. Finish with another drizzle of your best extra virgin olive oil and serve.

A MEZZE PLATTER

Often, when the sun has failed to shine and outdoor activities have been curtailed, I have been known to have **indoor picnics for friends** in the living room, with a bright tablecloth spread out on the floor and an exotic mezze platter *evoking a magic carpet ride* to far off – and much sunnier – climes… Make sure you have some really good olives in bowls, both green and black, some carrots, leaves of bitter endive, radishes and, of course, some lovely fresh pita or lavash bread. Each of these dishes serves about 12 but, all together, this is easily enough food for plenty more guests.

1 PARSLEY SALAD

Full of Mediterranean flavours, this salad is perfect for scooping up with bread.

SERVES 12

75 g (3 oz) flat leaf parsley, finely chopped

1 red onion, finely chopped

2 tbsp capers, drained and chopped

2 tbsp black olives, finely chopped

1 garlic clove, finely chopped

1 mild red chilli, deseeded and chopped (optional)

75 ml (3 fl oz) extra virgin olive oil

juice and finely grated rind of ½ lemon

sea salt and freshly ground black pepper

To garnish:

2 tbsp pomegranate seeds

½ tsp ground sumac

Place the parsley, onion, capers, olives, garlic and chilli, if using, in a large bowl and mix well. Stir in the olive oil, lemon juice and grated rind and season with salt and pepper. Leave to rest at room temperature for 30 minutes to 1 hour before serving, sprinkled with the pomegranate seeds and sumac.

2 LABNEH

Rich and creamy, cool and garlicky.

SERVES 12

500 g (1lb) Greek yogurt

2 garlic cloves, crushed

sea salt and freshly ground black pepper

To garnish:

extra virgin olive oil

1 tsp za'atar spice mix

Rest a sieve over a bowl, line it with muslin or a clean tea towel and pour in the yogurt. Twist the cloth at the top to cover the yogurt, then place in the refrigerator for 24 hours, squeezing the top of the cloth every now and then: you want to drain off the liquid.

Transfer the drained yogurt to a bowl and mash in the garlic, salt and pepper. Serve drizzled with extra virgin olive oil and sprinkled with the za'atar.

3 ROASTED RED PEPPER SALAD

Colourful and oh, so tasty!

SERVES 12

6 red peppers

3–4 tbsp extra virgin olive oil

leaves from a few thyme sprigs

sea salt and freshly ground black pepper

Hold the peppers, one at a time, over a gas flame, turning from time to time until they are charred and blackened all over. Alternatively, char them under a hot grill. Transfer to a bowl, cover with clingfilm (plastic wrap) and leave for about 30 minutes – the steam will make the roasted peppers easier to peel.

Once they are cool enough to handle, gently peel off the skins, then quarter the peppers lengthways and remove the cores and seeds. Arrange on a plate and dress with the olive oil and thyme leaves. Season with salt and pepper.

For a picture of these recipes, see pages 174–5

4 QUICK HUMMUS

Garlicky, lemony hummus is always a hit.

SERVES 12

2 x 400 g (13 oz) cans chickpeas, rinsed and drained

2 tbsp tahini

2 garlic cloves, chopped

a good pinch of ground cumin

2 tbsp lemon juice

a good splash of extra virgin olive oil, plus extra to garnish

150–200 ml (5–7 fl oz) warm water

sea salt and freshly ground black pepper

To garnish:

pinch of cayenne pepper or ground sumac

deep-fried garlic slices (optional)

Place the chickpeas, tahini, garlic, cumin, lemon juice and olive oil in a blender or food processor and blend until smooth. Add enough of the warm water, a little at a time, to give the hummus a smooth consistency. Season with salt and pepper.

Scoop it into a bowl and serve at room temperature, garnished with a sprinkling of cayenne pepper or sumac, a drizzle of olive oil and some fried garlic, if liked.

For a picture of this recipe, see page 175

NUTS

For Salted Almonds,
see page 33

Nuts, nuts, my kingdom for some nuts! Well, not quite...but they really ARE superb with a cocktail. There are no portion sizes here. I've seen these devoured by very few and (strangely) ignored by many. So *I leave it to your judgement.*

ROSEMARY AND CHILLI ROASTED WALNUTS

200 g (7 oz) walnut halves

½ tbsp olive oil

½ tbsp unsalted butter

leaves from 1 small rosemary sprig, finely chopped, plus extra to garnish

2 tsp caster (superfine) sugar

1 tsp cayenne pepper

sea salt

Preheat the oven to 180°C/350°F/Gas Mark 4. Spread the walnuts out on a baking sheet and toast in the oven for 5–8 minutes or until crisp. Keep an eye on them as they burn quickly. Remove from the oven and set aside.

Heat the olive oil and butter in a frying pan over a medium heat and, when the butter has melted, add the rosemary, sugar and cayenne pepper. Stir until the ingredients are well combined and the sugar has melted.

Add the walnuts and stir to coat thoroughly.

Remove from the heat, transfer to a bowl, add a good pinch of sea salt and mix again. Allow to cool slightly and serve with a sprinkle of extra salt and rosemary.

For a picture of this recipe, see page 137

PAYON'S PEANUTS

You can put these together in minutes – so no excuses.

200 g (7 oz) salted peanuts

½ lime, cut into tiny slivers

2 spring onions, green part only, finely chopped

1 large red chilli, deseeded and finely chopped

Mix all the ingredients together in a small bowl. Serve at once.

For a picture of this recipe, see page 118

VEGETABLES, GRAINS & DAIRY
TAYLOR'S-STYLE HOMEMADE POTATO CHIPS

At Taylor's Steakhouse in Los Angeles, not only do they grill up a fine T-bone ('charred and rare'), but they make the wait remarkably enjoyable by serving warm, straight-from-the-fryer salted crisps with one's aperitif. **Keeping it classy.** These are my homage…

500 g (1 lb) potatoes

1 litre (1¾ pints) vegetable oil

a good pinch of sea salt

a pinch of paprika (optional)

Peel the potatoes, then slice them very thinly, ideally with a mandolin. Soak the sliced potatoes in a bowl of cold water for 10 minutes to remove the starch. Drain, then spread out on a clean tea towel to dry thoroughly.

Heat the oil in a saucepan until very hot – it is ready when a cube of bread browns in just under a minute. Fry the chips in batches in the oil until they just turn golden brown, then remove them IMMEDIATELY to drain on paper towels. Note that if you put in too many at once, they will cool the oil and they won't cook properly.

Finally, sprinkle the chips with a good pinch of sea salt and dust with paprika, if you want to.

CHEDDAR-PARMESAN BISCUITS

These delicious cheesy biscuits are a complete doddle to make. They're **heavenly with a Dry Martini or a Champagne Cocktail**... in fact with just about any cocktail. And, while they're delicious cold, these are extra special when they're warm from the oven.

MAKES 24

125 g (4 oz) plain flour, plus extra for dusting

65 g (2½ oz) cold unsalted butter, cut into cubes

30 g (1¼ oz) Cheddar cheese, grated

30 g (1¼ oz) Parmesan cheese, grated

1 large egg yolk

a large pinch of cayenne pepper, plus extra to garnish

sea salt and freshly ground black pepper

Preheat the oven to 170°C/325°F/Gas Mark 3½. Place the flour in a large bowl and rub in the butter with your fingertips until the mixture resembles fine breadcrumbs. Stir in the grated cheeses, the egg yolk, the cayenne, a good pinch of sea salt and several good grindings of black pepper. Mix well with your hands until the mixture comes together into a dough. If it seems too dry, add a splash of cold water – but just a little.

Roll out the dough on a lightly floured, cool work surface to a thickness of about 5 mm (¼ inch). Cut out 24 biscuits using a 5 cm (2 inch) fluted pastry cutter and arrange on a baking sheet lined with baking parchment. Bake for 20 minutes until lightly golden and crisp. Serve warm, straight out of the oven, if possible. Sprinkle with a little extra cayenne, if you like.

For a picture of this dish, see page 128

LOU CACHAT

Let's face it, this is not so much a recipe as a **Provençal tradition** – a way of using up leftover cheese, all chopped up and squished together. Pungent but perfect, this is *at its best after a day in the fridge.*

SERVES 8–12

3 garlic cloves, peeled

400–500 g (13 oz–1 lb) leftover soft cheese (goats' and sheep' cheeses are particularly good)

a good pinch of thyme leaves

leaves from 1 rosemary sprig

2 tbsp eau de vie, brandy or Calvados

sea salt and freshly ground black pepper

chunks of baguette, to serve

Use a pestle and mortar to crush the garlic with a little sea salt to form a smooth paste. Add the cheeses and mash them together. Add the herbs, alcohol and some pepper, then blend together until smooth. You may find a large fork or potato masher handy. Put the mixture into a jam jar or mason jar, cover and refrigerate until needed.

Take the Lou Cachat out of the refrigerator at least 30 minutes before you want it, and serve it in its jar with chunks of baguette.

TAPENADE

Laden with Provençal flavours, this garlicky tapenade should be used sparingly! Serve with crudités, fresh bread or crisp slices of baguette that you have toasted in the oven. Any leftovers are **delicious smothered on lamb** before roasting or barbecuing.

MAKES ABOUT 300 ML (½ PINT)

300 g (10 oz) pitted black olives

6 tbsp capers, rinsed

leaves from 1 large rosemary sprig

8 garlic cloves, chopped

6–8 tbsp olive oil

50 g (2 oz) drained canned anchovies in olive oil (optional)

1 tbsp brandy

juice of ½ lemon

sea salt and freshly ground black pepper

Place all the ingredients in a blender or food processor and blend until well combined but still retaining some texture. Taste and add more lemon juice or adjust the seasoning if necessary. Serve straightaway, or keep tightly covered in the refrigerator until needed. It will keep for one week.

ARANCINI

These deep-fried balls of risotto have a **hidden centre** of gooey, melted mozzarella. Serve on their own or with a piquant tomato dip for one of the **most decadent snacks going**… You will need to make the risotto the day before you want to serve them.

MAKES 36

1.2 litres (2 pints) chicken or vegetable stock

1 tbsp olive oil

20 g (¾ oz) butter

1 onion, finely chopped

1 garlic clove, finely chopped

250 g (8 oz) arborio rice

100 ml (3½ fl oz) white wine

1 tbsp grated Parmesan cheese

2 tbsp finely chopped parsley

finely grated rind of ½ lemon

3 eggs

1 tbsp lemon juice (optional)

50 g (2 oz) plain flour

125 g (4 oz) fresh breadcrumbs

75 g (3 oz) mozzarella cheese, cut into 36 pieces

vegetable oil, for deep-frying

Tomato and Basil Dip (see opposite), to serve (optional)

First make the risotto. Bring the stock to the boil in a saucepan over a high heat, then reduce the heat and keep it at a gentle simmer. Heat the oil and melt the butter in it over a low to medium heat in a second saucepan, add the onion and cook gently until translucent. Add the garlic and cook for another minute or so, then add the rice and stir until it is well coated.

Add the wine, turn up the heat and stir the rice until almost all the wine has been absorbed. Now add a ladleful of stock. Stir the rice, cooking it over a medium heat until most of the stock has been absorbed, then add more stock, being careful not to flood the rice at any time, and cook, stirring, until it has been absorbed again. Keep adding stock and absorbing it into the rice until the rice is cooked to the texture you like. You will probably have a little stock leftover.

When the rice is done, season with salt and pepper, then stir in the Parmesan, parsley and lemon rind. Stir thoroughly, then set aside to cool. Refrigerate for up to 2 days until ready to make the arancini.

To make the arancini, break one of the eggs into the risotto and stir in thoroughly, followed by the lemon juice, if using. It gives the arancini an extra citrus bounce.

For a picture of this dish,
see page 128

Now prepare a three-stage breadcrumbing area: place the flour in one bowl and season with salt and pepper. Place the breadcrumbs in another bowl and beat the remaining eggs in a third bowl.

With cool and slightly damp hands, roll the risotto into about 36 balls the size of a large walnut. Flatten them slightly in your palm and push a piece of mozzarella into each one. Then shape them back into balls, enclosing the cheese. You may need to refrigerate the arancini between steps if they become too sticky.

One at a time, roll the risotto balls in the flour to coat, shaking off the excess, then in the beaten egg and, finally, in the breadcrumbs. Place the balls on a baking sheet lined with baking paper.

Heat the oil for deep-frying in a saucepan until very hot – it is ready when a cube of bread browns in just under a minute. Deep-fry the arancini, a few at a time, for 3–4 minutes until crisp and golden. Drain on paper towels and serve with sticks or small forks, with Tomato and Basil Dip (see below), if liked.

TOMATO AND BASIL DIP

1 tbsp olive oil

1 onion, finely chopped

2 garlic cloves, chopped

400 g (13 oz) can chopped tomatoes

1 tbsp tomato purée

1 teaspoon dried oregano

a handful of basil leaves, torn into small pieces

sea salt and freshly ground black pepper

Heat the olive oil in a saucepan over a medium heat, add the onion and cook until soft. Add the garlic and cook for another couple of minutes or so, then add the tomatoes. Stir in the tomato purée and oregano, and season with salt and pepper. Cook until the sauce is thick and reduced.

Stir in the basil then set aside to cool completely. Serve in a bowl alongside the arancini.

TOMATOES AND SALT, AND BUTTERED RADISHES

Canapés do not need to be complicated. In fact, **the simplest things are often the best.** And what could be simpler or indeed more naturally beautiful than this pair of summer delights? Look for different colours and varieties of tomatoes (I've always been a big fan of heirloom tomatoes), and try to find French breakfast radishes with their elegant lines and sweeping green tops. They are **utterly delicious.** So think of this not so much as a recipe, because it's not: it's an idea, the vegetable version of a plate of perfect ham. Better still, you don't have to worry about portions – *you can serve as few or as many as you like!*

TOMATOES

lots of little ripe tomatoes, at room temperature

coarse sea salt or sel de gris

Put bowls or plates of tomatoes around the room, accompanied by the salt.

BUTTERED RADISHES

several bunches of radishes, trimmed but with some of their tops left on

good unsalted butter, softened

coarse sea salt or sel de gris

Lay out the radishes on platters, accompanied by pillowy mounds of softened butter and small piles of salt. To eat, dunk the radishes into the butter, then into the salt.

KAY'S TIP: You could ring the changes by beating some chopped herbs such as parsley or chervil and thyme into the butter to accompany the radishes.

QUAILS' EGGS WITH CELERY SALT, CUMIN AND BLACK PEPPER

Sophisticated but oh, so simple! The secret is to get the eggs just so – you want a little glossy 'give' in the yolk, but for the white to be firm. Enlist help with the peeling over a glass of something cool…

MAKES 24

24 quails' eggs

2 tbsp sea salt

1 tsp freshly ground black pepper

1 tsp ground cumin

Check the eggs over and discard any that are broken or cracked. Bring a saucepan of salted water to a rolling boil. Gently lower the eggs into the water – I use a slotted spoon – and boil for 2½–3 minutes. You may need to do this in 2 or 3 batches to avoid overcrowding the pan, which will lower the water temperature too much and affect cooking.

Remove the eggs from the pan and plunge immediately into a large bowl of ice-cold water. Allow to cool completely, then carefully peel them. Mix the salt, pepper and cumin together and serve in little piles alongside the eggs. If you have any cumin salt left over, keep it in a container and use it as a condiment – it's delicious.

 For a picture of this dish, see page 117

POTATO, MANCHEGO AND SAFFRON TORTILLA

Golden morsels of eggy delight, wafting the scent of saffron and warm Spanish evenings through your home.

SERVES 8

4 eggs

a pinch of saffron threads

50 g (2 oz) Manchego cheese, grated

75 g (3 oz) new potatoes

2 tablespoons olive oil

sea salt and freshly ground black pepper

Break the eggs into a bowl, add the saffron and beat lightly. Add salt and pepper to taste and the Manchego, stir through and set aside.

Place the potatoes in a saucepan of lightly salted water and bring to the boil. Simmer for 8–10 minutes until JUST cooked, then remove from the heat, drain and refresh in cold water. Drain again and set aside to dry thoroughly, then cut into 5mm (¼ inch) thick slices.

Heat the oil in a small tortilla pan or frying pan, about 16cm (6¼ inches) across with a heatproof handle. Add the potatoes and cook for a few minutes, turning now and then, until golden and soft. You may have to do this in batches.

Pour the eggs over the potatoes and cook gently to set, using a spatula to pull back the edges to check that it's browning nicely underneath.

When the bottom and sides are golden, and only the top has yet to set, place the pan under a preheated hot grill and cook until golden and puffy. Allow to cool slightly, then turn out on to a plate and scatter over some shavings of Manchego, if you like. Cut into wedges and serve warm or cold.

For a picture of this dish,
see page 112

FISH & SEAFOOD
VODKA & CARAWAY CURED SALMON

A Lithuanian take on the traditional Scandinavian gravadlax. The vodka and caraway make for a delicious combination, and the beetroot pickle lends a fresh tartness. Try it with chilled shots of good vodka, a Gimlet (see page 45) or the Modern Mad Men on page 67. Don't forget to start two days before you want to eat it.

MAKES 35 CANAPÉS, OR 12–16 LARGER PORTIONS

1 kg (2lb) very fresh, centre-cut salmon fillet

2 tsp black peppercorns, crushed

½ heaped tbsp caraway seeds, lightly crushed

75 g (3 oz) Maldon sea salt

75 g (3 oz) caster (superfine) sugar

75 ml (3 fl oz) vodka

20 g (¾ oz) dill, chopped, plus extra to garnish

To serve:

Quick Beetroot Pickle (see page 192) or lemon wedges

rye bread

Cut the salmon in half across the fillet, remove any pin bones and set aside on a board, skin-side down.

Place the crushed peppercorns in a bowl with the caraway seeds, salt and sugar. Then mix in the vodka. Evenly spread the mixture on to the flesh side of the salmon, pressing it in until you have used it all up. Lay the dill evenly over the surface of the fish. Now sandwich the two pieces of salmon together, skin-side out, so that the curing sides are touching each other. Tie with string, tucking in any filling which spills out, then wrap the fish tightly in clingfilm (plastic wrap) – I like to wrap it twice so it is really secure.

Place the parcel in a dish to catch any escaping liquids, and refrigerate for 48 hours. You can weight the salmon down with something heavy if you like. And, if you remember, you can turn it a couple of times, but it doesn't really make that much difference.

Remove the salmon from the clingfilm (plastic wrap) and gently wipe off the excess dill and cure. Place the fish skin-side down on a board and scatter with a little extra dill.

Serve the salmon with the beetroot pickle on the side and slices of good rye bread. Or assemble the canapés yourself by thinly slicing the salmon, placing it on rye bread, and topping it with a little of the pickle. You could also serve it with lemon wedges instead.

QUICK
BEETROOT
PICKLE

2 small raw beetroots, grated

2 tbsp red wine vinegar

2 tbsp olive oil

sea salt and freshly ground black
pepper

Place all the ingredients in a
large bowl and leave for about
2 hours. Then drain off the liquid
thoroughly before serving the
grated beetroot with the salmon.
This can be made a few hours
before you want to serve it.

POTTED SHRIMPS ON TOAST

How much more British seaside can you get than simple yet **delicious buttery shrimps,** redolent with woody spices?

MAKES 26–32

160 g (5½ oz) unsalted butter

a good pinch of grated nutmeg

2 large pinches of ground mace

a good pinch of cayenne pepper

1 bay leaf

juice of ½ lemon

200 g (7 oz) cooked and peeled brown shrimps

sea salt and freshly ground white pepper

hot toast, cut into triangles, to serve

Melt the butter in a saucepan over a low heat until the solids start to separate – you want to clarify it. Once you have achieved this, strain off the clarified butter into a clean bowl, discarding the white residue or solids. Set aside 3 tbsp of the clarified butter and keep warm. Wipe out the saucepan and pour in the remaining clarified butter. Add the spices, bay leaf, lemon juice and shrimps to the pan. Season with salt, pepper and cayenne pepper. Bring to a gentle simmer then immediately take off the heat and stir well. Set aside to cool a little.

Remove the bay leaf, then scoop the shrimps into a bowl or jar and pat down firmly. Place the bay leaf on top and pour over the reserved clarified butter. Cover and refrigerate at least 3 hours. Remove from the fridge a few minutes before serving. Serve with a teaspoon and wee triangles of toast.

COCKLES & BROWN SHRIMP

When I was a girl, I used to accompany my grandfather to the Brockley Jack pub on a Saturday morning to get my fill of old-fashioned seafood: cockles, whelks, mussels, you name it – delicious tidbits of shellfish served with a dash of malt vinegar and lashings of white pepper. Just gorgeous. How wonderful that, as an adult, I discovered that they are an admirable companion to a few pre-dinner drinks!

If you can find a stack of paper cups and some wooden cocktail forks or chip sticks to serve, *this makes for a nostalgic and very attractive canapé.*

SERVES 12–16

250 g (8 oz) cooked and peeled brown shrimps

250 g (8 oz) shelled and cooked cockles

malt vinegar or white wine vinegar, to serve

freshly ground white pepper

Divide the cockles and brown shrimps evenly between 12–16 cups or small bowls. Douse them liberally with vinegar and season with plenty of white pepper. Serve with sticks or forks.

KAY'S TIP: You could replace the brown shrimps and cockles with equal quantities of shelled mussels, clams or whelks. The weights will vary, but you're looking for portions of approximately 25 g (1 oz) a cup.

NOT QUITE MARYLAND CRAB CAKES

Crab cakes always get a reaction – I've been at events where people throng at the doors to the kitchens just to **snaffle them fresh off the serving plates.** But I can never decide between the classic Maryland version or something a little more Cajun. This is a bit of a compromise between the two.

MAKES ABOUT 36

1 egg

2 tsp Worcestershire sauce

¼ tsp mustard powder

2 tbsp mayonnaise

finely grated rind of ½ lemon

1 tsp lemon juice

½–1 tsp cayenne pepper

1 tbsp Dijon mustard

25 g (1 oz) butter, melted

1 tbsp chopped parsley

1 heaped tsp Old Bay Seasoning

50 g (2 oz) crushed Ritz crackers

500 g (1 lb) good-quality crab meat

4 tbsp vegetable oil

Chipotle Mayonnaise (see page 198) or Horseradish Mayonnaise (see page 198), to serve

Place the egg in a mixing bowl with the Worcestershire sauce, mustard powder, mayonnaise, lemon rind and juice, cayenne, Dijon mustard, melted butter, parsley, Old Bay Seasoning and crushed crackers and mix well to combine. Then gently fold in the crab meat, being careful not to break up the lumps.

Shape the mixture into about 36 small patties and place on a baking sheet lined with baking parchment. Refrigerate for about 30 minutes to firm up the patties a little.

Heat the oil in a large nonstick frying pan until hot and fry the crab cakes, a few at a time, for 5–6 minutes, turning them gently, until golden brown and cooked through. Drain on paper towels and serve with cocktail forks, with one or both of the flavoured mayonnaises for dipping.

Note: More of a confession than a note, but this recipe works perfectly well with tinned crab! It also halves perfectly, so I'll sometimes whip up a half-batch with tinned crab for a quick kitchen supper.

Chipotle Mayonnaise
see page 198

CHIPOTLE MAYONNAISE

1 chipotle chilli in adobo sauce

3 heaped tbsp good-quality mayonnaise

a dash of lemon juice

Purée the chipotle chilli and a little sauce from the jar using a hand blender. Mix 2 tsp of the paste with the mayonnaise and lemon juice. Serve with the crab cakes on page 196.

HORSERADISH MAYONNAISE

3 heaped tbsp good-quality mayonnaise

1–2 tbsp fresh grated horseradish

8 cornichons, chopped

1 tbsp capers, rinsed

a dash of lemon juice

Mix all the ingredients together and serve with the crab cakes on page 196.

CEVICHE SHOTS

Briny, spicy, citrus-fresh seafood served in shot glasses, these can be made comfortably ahead of time and served up super-quick. Which makes them perfect for party food, when you don't want to spend a lot of time in the kitchen away from your friends. *Plus they're sassy and contemporary, and you can never go wrong with that.*

SERVES 12–16

250 g (8 oz) boneless, skinless firm white fish (monkfish, haddock or tilapia), cut into small chunks

250 g (8 oz) raw peeled prawns, chopped

200 ml (7 fl oz) lime juice, plus an extra dash to taste

2 garlic cloves, finely chopped

1 Serrano or ½ Habanero chilli, deseeded and finely chopped

3 tomatoes, finely chopped

a good pinch of dried oregano

1 orange pepper, cored, deseeded and finely diced

1 red onion, finely chopped

4–6 dashes of hot sauce (Tabasco, Grace or Crystal), plus extra to serve

2 avocados, finely diced

2 tbsp chopped fresh coriander (cilantro)

sea salt

lime wedges, to serve

Place the fish and prawns in a non-metallic bowl and add the lime juice, garlic and chilli. Cover with clingfilm (plastic wrap) and refrigerate for 2–4 hours. The seafood will 'cook' in the acid of the lime juice.

Strain the fish and prawns thoroughly and transfer to a clean bowl. Add the tomatoes, oregano, orange pepper and red onion and mix together gently. Cover and refrigerate for another 20 minutes.

Taste the ceviche and add a dash more lime juice, some salt and the hot sauce, to taste. Add the avocado and coriander and stir through gently. Divide the mixture between the shot glasses and serve with lime wedges and some hot sauce on the side.

For a picture of this dish, see page 89

CRAB, SAFFRON AND GRUYÈRE TART

This is, essentially, a quiche that has grown up and moved abroad...**sophisticated, creamy and fragrant with saffron.** It's best served at just above room temperature – definitely not cold – so it still has *a little wobble and warmth.*

SERVES 12

2 eggs plus 1 egg yolk, lightly beaten

200 ml (7 fl oz) double (heavy) cream

a pinch of grated nutmeg

a large pinch of saffron threads

170 g can crab meat, drained

100 g (3½ oz) Gruyère cheese, grated

sea salt and freshly ground black pepper

Pastry:

225 g (7½ oz) plain flour

110 g (3¾ oz) cold unsalted butter

a small glass of iced water

Preheat the oven to 190°C/375°F/Gas Mark 5 and grease a 20 cm (8 inch) round or 36 x12 cm (14 x 4½ inch) rectangular loose-bottomed flan tin.

To make the pastry, sift the flour into a mixing bowl, then chop the fridge-cold butter into small pieces and drop them into the bowl. Coat them in flour, then rub the butter and flour between your fingertips, lifting it, rubbing it together until the mixture resembles fine breadcrumbs. Add a good pinch of salt and stir it in. Then add the iced water, a teaspoonful at a time, until the pastry just comes together. If you add too much water you'll get a hard pastry.

Push the pastry straight into the greased flan tin, easing it around gently with your knuckles until it is evenly covering the base and sides. Line the pastry case with baking parchment and weight it down with baking beans. Bake blind for about 10 minutes, then remove the beans and paper and return the tart case to the oven for a further 5 minutes. Set aside to cool.

To make the filling, mix the eggs and the yolk, the cream, nutmeg and saffron in a large bowl and season with salt and pepper. Beat the mixture with a hand-held electric whisk to combine thoroughly, then leave to stand for 20 minutes. Beat again, then carefully stir in the crab and grated cheese.

Pour the filing into the flan tin and bake for 30–40 minutes until the pastry is golden brown and the filling is domed, burnished and puffy. Allow to cool to room temperature, or just above, before serving.

FIG ANCHOIADE

This is based on a delicious dip made famous by early twentieth-century food writer Austin de Croze, which I discovered in a French cookbook many years ago. **It is utterly magical**…and your friends will not believe what's in it.

SERVES 12–16

5 dried figs

1 red pepper

110 g (4 oz) drained canned anchovies in olive oil

3 garlic cloves, peeled

20 g (¾ oz) blanched almonds

75 g (3 oz) walnuts

a handful of flat leaf parsley

a handful of fresh coriander (cilantro)

½ tsp fennel seeds

juice of ½ lemon

½ Apache or small hot red chilli or a pinch of dried chilli flakes

150 ml (¼ pint) extra virgin olive oil

1–2 tsp orange flower water

a capful of Pastis or Herbsaint

freshly ground black pepper

toast or crudités, to serve

Soak the figs in a bowl of hot water for about 10 minutes to rehydrate. Hold the red pepper over a gas flame, turning from time to time, until it is charred and blackened all over. Alternatively, char it under a hot grill. Transfer to a bowl, cover with clingfilm (plastic wrap) and leave for about 30 minutes – the steam will make it easier to peel.

Once it is cool enough to handle, gently peel off the skin and remove the core and seeds.

Put everything except the oil and orange flower water into a blender or food processor and blend until smooth, adding in the oil in a gentle but steady stream as the machine works until it's well combined. Season with pepper, then add the orange flower water a spoonful at a time, tasting as you go – you don't want it too perfumed.

And that's it! Let the anchoiade mature a little before serving at room temperature with small triangles of toast or a selection of crudités. This will keep, covered in the refrigerator, for up to 5 days – the flavour just keeps getting better and better.

STAMP 'N' GO

You'll often find these Jamaican salt cod fishcakes served for breakfast, maybe with some fried plantain on the side. But I think they make **a first-rate canapé,** too, especially with a small bowl of your favourite hot sauce for dipping.

MAKES ABOUT 24

250 g (8 oz) salt cod or other salt fish

125 g (4 oz) plain flour

1 tsp baking powder

a large pinch of sea salt

200 ml (7 fl oz) buttermilk

1 large egg, beaten

20 g (¾ oz) butter, melted

4 large spring onions, finely chopped

½–1 Scotch Bonnet chilli, deseeded and finely chopped

2 tbsp vegetable oil

freshly ground black pepper

hot sauce, for dipping

Place the salt fish in a large bowl of warm water and soak for at least 2 hours to soften it and remove the salt. Note that it may take longer, depending on how hard and salty your piece of fish is. Drain and rinse the fish, then put it in a saucepan with enough fresh water to cover it. Bring it to a simmer, then cook for about 15 minutes, until tender. Shred the fish, removing any skin and bones.

Sift the flour, baking powder and salt into a bowl. In a separate bowl, mix the buttermilk, egg and melted butter, then stir them into the dry ingredients. Add the fish, spring onions and chilli, season with pepper and mix together well.

Heat the oil in a nonstick frying pan over a high heat. Shape tablespoonfuls of the mixture into small patties using your hands and place, a few at a time, in the hot pan. Cook until golden brown on both sides, then drain on paper towels and serve hot with hot sauce for dipping.

OYSTERS ON THE HALF SHELL WITH TWO MIGNONETTES

Why mess with perfection? There's nothing better than a briny, creamy, spankingly fresh oyster, served simply with a wedge of lemon and some Tabasco, or with one or both of the mignonettes below. Speaking of which, it goes without saying that **you want your oysters to be as fresh as possible.** So, if you feel confident about shucking them, it's best to buy them whole from your fishmonger or dedicated supplier (I'm a big fan of Richard Haward's oysters from West Mersea). Just make sure you have a proper oyster knife. If not, you can ask your fishmonger to open them for you. Each sauce is enough for 24 oysters.

1 SIMPLE MIGNONETTE

An absolute classic accompaniment to raw oysters – spoon over the oysters at will. Feel free to change the vinegar to one of your favourites, or to combine a couple – sherry vinegar is wonderful with some extra parsley, and rice wine vinegar works beautifully with a little wasabi stirred in.

75 ml (3 fl oz) red wine vinegar

3 tbsp very finely chopped shallots

½–1 tsp freshly ground black pepper

a pinch of salt

Combine the ingredients and leave to macerate for at least 2 hours before serving.

2 MEE'S MIGNONETTE

From my friend Somjai Kliangklom in Southern Thailand – home to some of the most delicious oysters I have ever eaten. This is **a stunner of a topping,** more of a construct than a sauce. A little warning: it BITES, *so deseed the chillies to reduce the heat if you like.*

6–8 bird's eye chillies

3 large garlic cloves, peeled

2 tbsp sugar

1 tsp Thai fish sauce (nam pla)

juice of 1–2 limes

To garnish:

oil, for deep-frying

6 Thai shallots or 2 regular shallots, thinly sliced

4 garlic cloves, very thinly sliced

2 limes, cut into segments with the membrane removed

24 kratin (horse tamarind) or fresh coriander (cilantro) sprigs

2–3 spring onions, finely sliced

Use a pestle and mortar to pound the chillies and garlic until smooth. Add the sugar and pound again. Add the fish sauce and the juice from 1 lime, stir well and taste the dressing, adding more lime juice if necessary. Set aside.

Heat the oil in a wok or frying pan over a medium heat. When it's hot, deep-fry the sliced shallots, moving them all the time, until golden and crispy. Drain on paper towels.

Serve the oysters with a drizzle of the mignonette, and garnished with a little bit of everything else.

Note: You can find kratin at most good Asian supermarkets. It's the most extraordinary herb and tastes amazing with shellfish.

For a picture of these dishes, see page 204

SMOKED SALMON AND DILL DEVILLED EGGS

How much more retro can you get than a cheeky devilled egg? It's a classic of this oeuvre (ouch!). I used to make dozens of these with my mum's great friend Shirley when she threw her annual Christmas extravaganza. Here is an updated version: smoked salmon with mustard and dill. ***Devilish indeed!***

MAKES 24

12 eggs, hard-boiled, cooled and peeled

4 tbsp sour cream

3 tsp English mustard

1 tsp grated horseradish

1 tbsp lemon juice

1 tbsp finely chopped dill, plus extra to garnish

25–30 g (1–1¼ oz) smoked salmon, cut into 24 pieces

sea salt and freshly ground black pepper

Carefully cut the eggs in half along their lengths, then scoop out the yolks into a large bowl and arrange the whites on a serving plate.

Add the sour cream, mustard, horseradish and lemon juice to the yolks and mash well together. Season with salt and plenty of pepper, then gently stir through the chopped dill. Taste and adjust the seasoning, if necessary, and if you feel it's a little dry, add a dash more soured cream.

Scoop or pipe the yolk mixture back into the egg white shells. Top with the slivers of smoked salmon, then sprinkle with a little more dill and a grinding of black pepper.

MINI LAARP LETTUCE ROLLS

Spicy, tart and fragrant, these canapés are **the perfect appetite-sharpener** to have with drinks before dinner.

MAKES 24–30

500 g (1 lb) boneless, skinless lean duck, finely chopped or minced

2 tbsp Thai fish sauce (nam pla)

3 tbsp lime juice

½–1 tsp roasted chilli powder

4 Thai shallots or 2 regular shallots, thinly sliced

1–2 tbsp ground toasted rice (see right)

a large handful of mint leaves, torn

1 lemon grass stalk, tough outer leaves removed, core thinly sliced (optional)

24–30 Baby Gem lettuce leaves

lime wedges, to serve

Bring a saucepan of water to the boil over a medium heat and add the duck. Bring back to the boil, and cook the duck to your liking: it will take just a minute or so for it to be pink, a bit longer if you want it done through. Bear in mind that people sometimes eat this raw!

Transfer the duck to a large bowl and add the fish sauce, lime juice, chilli powder, shallots, ground rice, mint and lemon grass, if using. Mix well.

Line a plate with Baby Gem lettuce leaves, spoon the laarp inside them and serve with lime wedges while still warm, if possible.

Note: You can buy ground toasted rice in Asian supermarkets or make your own. To make your own, take a large handful of uncooked sticky rice (or normal Thai jasmine rice, if necessary) and place it in a dry wok or frying pan over a low heat. Toast the rice, moving it all the time, until it smells nutty and has turned a dark golden brown. Grind it in a spice or coffee grinder, or in a pestle and mortar. Store in a jar and use as required.

CHICKEN LIVER PATÉ WITH APPLES, SAGE AND CALVADOS

Creamy and rich **with a tang of apple,** this is a winner at any event. Serve with crisp toast points or chunks of fresh French bread.

SERVES 24

750 g (1½ lb) chicken livers

200 g (7 oz) butter

2 tbsp olive oil

4 apples (preferably Cox's), peeled, cored and cut into chunks

8 sage leaves, roughly torn, plus 2 more to garnish

4 tbsp Calvados or brandy

250 ml (8 fl oz) double (heavy) cream

sea salt and freshly ground black pepper

To serve:

slices of baguette

cornichons and pickled onions

Pick over the chicken livers and remove any fat, gristle or green bits. Then chop them into bite-size pieces and set aside.

Heat 50 g (2 oz) of the butter and half the olive oil in a nonstick frying pan over a medium heat until the butter foams, then add the apples. Sauté them for 5–10 minutes until golden and soft. You want the wooden spoon to cut through them with ease. Transfer to a plate and set aside.

Season the livers and heat another 50 g (2 oz) of the butter and the remaining olive oil in the pan and, when it's hot, add the livers. (You may have to do this in batches, depending on the size of your pan.) Cook the livers through (no pink bits in this recipe) – it could take anywhere from 10–15 minutes. Just keep prodding them until the juices run clear.

Return the apples to the pan, add the sage and combine well, letting it all bubble. Add another 25 g (1 oz) of butter and stir it through until it is melted and bubbling.

Now carefully add half the Calvados and flambé by lighting the alcohol fumes with a match. Take it off the heat and let the flames die.

Set aside to cool for 5–10 minutes, then transfer the mixture to a blender or food processor and blend, adding the cream slowly while the machine is running. Stop now and then to scrape down the sides and check the consistency – we want creamy with a little texture. Add the remaining Calvados and pulse briefly or stir in. Season with salt and pepper to taste.

Pour the paté into a bowl or a mason jar and cool before covering the surface with a round of greaseproof paper. Place in the refrigerator to chill. Once it's cold, melt the remaining butter in a small pan and set aside to allow the white solids to fall to the bottom. Arrange 2 sage leaves artfully in the middle of the paté, then pour over the clear clarified butter, leaving the white solids in the bottom of the pan. Cover and refrigerate until ready to serve. The paté will keep for 4–5 days.

> **KAY'S TIP:** This also works beautifully with the same amounts of duck livers, pears and Poire William liqueur.

PARMESAN CRISPS WITH BEEF CARPACCIO AND ROCKET

Crisp, salty, sharp discs of cheese with a pile of rare beef nestled on top and capped off with a **punchy horseradish cream** – these little bites are perfect foils to the drier drinks: a Martini, a Vesper, or a glass of Champagne…

MAKES ABOUT 24

250 g (8 oz) piece of fillet steak

1 tbsp olive oil

a good handful of rocket (arugula)

sea salt and freshly ground black pepper

lemon wedges, to serve

Parmesan crisps:

125 g (4 oz) Parmesan cheese, finely grated

finely grated rind of 1 lemon

1–2 tsp thyme leaves

Horseradish cream:

2 tsp grated horseradish

4 tsp soured cream

a squeeze of lemon juice

To make the Parmesan crisps, preheat the oven to 180°C/350°F/Gas Mark 4. Place all the ingredients in a bowl, season well with black pepper and mix gently until well combined. Line a baking sheet with a silicone liner or baking parchment. If you only have greaseproof paper, make sure you grease it. Place a 6.5 cm (2¾ inch) pastry cutter on the baking sheet and sprinkle a heaped tablespoonful of the cheese mixture into it. Even out the cheese a little, but don't flatten it entirely. Repeat to make 24 rounds of cheese, spacing them a little apart on the baking sheet.

Bake for 4–6 minutes, until golden and melted. Be careful not to burn them. Transfer the Parmesan crisps to a wire rack to cool and set aside until needed, or store in an airtight container overnight.

To cook the beef, heat a nonstick griddle or frying pan over a high heat. Rub both sides of the beef fillet with olive oil, and season it thoroughly with salt and pepper. Cook the beef in the hot pan for 2–3 minutes on each side until seared on the outside but still very rare inside. Transfer to a plate and leave to rest for 10–15 minutes, then refrigerate until it is completely cold. This will make the beef easier to slice.

To make the horseradish cream, place all the ingredients in a small bowl, season with salt and pepper and mix together thoroughly.

To assemble the canapés, slice the beef very thinly. Place a rolled-up slice on top of each Parmesan crisp and top with a little horseradish cream and a couple of leaves of rocket (arugula). Serve with lemon wedges on the side.

For a picture of this dish,

see page 39

PORK CRACKLING WITH ROSEMARY AND FENNEL

This is worlds away from the tooth-shattering scratchings you find in foil bags in the pub! Make sure the pork skin is very dry before cooking. If it is at all damp, it will NOT crackle. I dry it thoroughly, then leave it uncovered in the fridge overnight. Serve still warm from the oven – **crispy, fragrant, salty** – for the perfect accompaniment to a cold drink.

MAKES ABOUT 24 PIECES

2 pieces of pork skin with fat still attached, about 25 x 25 cm (10 x 10 inches) in total, scored

1 large rosemary sprig

1 tsp fennel seeds

½–1 tbsp olive oil

a good pinch of sea salt

Preheat the oven to 200°C/400°F/Gas Mark 6. Trim the fat on the back of the pork skin to form an even layer 5–10 mm (¼–½ inch) thick.

Strip the leaves from the rosemary sprig and spread them on a baking sheet with the fennel seeds. Lay the skin, fat-side down, on top. Pour the olive oil on the skin and rub it in well. Sprinkle the salt over the top and rub it in, too, making sure it goes into the score marks.

Bake for 35 minutes, then check to see if it has crackled properly. If not, drain off any excess fat and return to the oven for another 5–10 minutes. When it's done, transfer to a wire rack over paper towels. Then, when it's cool enough to handle, break it into strips and serve immediately.

For a picture of this dish,
see page 41

FRENCH-TRIMMED LAMB CUTLETS WITH SALSA VERDE

Juicy lamb chops and a punchy, herb-laden dip make for an elegant and tasty canapé – ideal for when there's just a few of you. Ask your butcher to French-trim the lamb cutlets so you have more of a 'bone handle' for your guests to hold on to. And *make the salsa verde a few hours ahead of time to let the flavours mingle.*

SERVES 24–32

4 racks of lamb, 6–8 cutlets per rack, French-trimmed

2 tablespoons olive oil

sea salt and freshly ground black pepper

Salsa verde:

6–8 garlic cloves

50 g (2 oz) drained canned anchovies in olive oil

2 tbsp capers, rinsed

a big handful of flat leaf parsley

a big handful of mint

a big handful of basil

juice of 1 lemon

1 tbsp red wine vinegar

6–8 tbsp olive oil

First make the salsa verde. Either place everything in a blender or food processor and pulse until it forms a sauce, or use a pestle and mortar. If using a pestle and mortar, start by crushing the garlic thoroughly. Chop the anchovies, add them to the mortar and rub them into the garlic. Then chop the capers and the herbs. Add them to the mortar and pound them into the anchovy-garlic paste. Add the lemon juice, vinegar and 6 tbsp of the olive oil, and stir into the mixture until you have an emulsified sauce, adding more oil if necessary. Season with salt and pepper to taste.

Rub the racks of lamb with a little of the oil, then season them very well with pepper. Leave to stand for about 30 minutes.

When you are ready to cook the lamb, preheat the oven to 200°C/400°F/Gas Mark 6. Heat the remaining olive oil in a large roasting pan over a medium heat. Season the racks with salt and sear them in the roasting pan, one at a time, on all sides until they're nicely brown. (Don't forget the ends!) Then place them all into the pan, fat-sides up, and roast in the oven for 15–20 minutes, depending on their weight, for a nice rosé finish.

Transfer to a warm plate and leave to rest for 8–10 minutes. Carve into single cutlets and serve with the salsa verde on the side.

STICKY SPICED CHICKEN WINGS

These are always a real favourite, **sticky and sweet** with a good punch of pepper and coriander. Just make sure you've plenty of napkins to go round – *there will be a lot of dirty fingers.*

MAKES 40 PIECES

20 chicken wings

1 tbsp vegetable oil

2 tbsp thick soy sauce or kecap manis

2 tbsp light soy sauce

2 tbsp caster (superfine) sugar

4–6 garlic cloves, finely chopped

½ tbsp coriander seeds, crushed

a dash of Thai fish sauce (nam pla) (optional)

freshly ground white pepper

Thai Peanut Brittle Dipping Sauce, to serve (see page 169)

Cut the chicken wings into their 3 separate joints and discard the tips or save them to make stock. Place the remaining 40 pieces in a large bowl.

Place all the remaining ingredients in a separate bowl and mix together. Pour the mixture over the chicken and toss thoroughly to coat. Leave to marinate for at least an hour.

When you're ready to cook, preheat the oven to 200°C/400°F/ Gas Mark 6. Lay the chicken pieces on a baking sheet and bake for about 30 minutes, turning once, until cooked through.

They should be sticky and delicious. Serve with Thai Peanut Brittle Dipping Sauce.

JERK CHICKEN AND FRESH MANGO SALSA POPPADUMS

A little mouthful of Caribbean sunshine. Beware: **they have a bite!**

MAKES 26–30

250 g (8 oz) boneless, skinless chicken thighs or breasts

1–2 tbsp good-quality jerk marinade

a squeeze of lime juice

26–30 mini poppadums

Mango salsa:

100 g (3½ oz) ripe mango, chopped

½ small red onion, finely chopped

1 tbsp chopped fresh coriander (cilantro)

1 red chilli, deseeded and chopped (optional)

juice of ½ lime

a pinch of sea salt

Place the chicken pieces in a large bowl, add the jerk marinade and lime juice, and leave to marinate for about an hour.

Preheat the oven to 180°C/350°F/Gas Mark 4. Transfer the chicken to a roasting pan and bake for 20–25 minutes or until cooked through. Set aside to cool.

Now make the salsa by gently mixing together all the ingredients and set aside.

Arrange the poppadums on a serving plate. Cut the chicken into 1 cm (½ inch) dice and pile a little on to each poppadum. Then top each with some mango salsa. Serve promptly.

KAY'S TIP: I favour the Walkerswood brand of jerk marinade – it's spiky and fiery, and contrasts beautifully with the sweetness of the mango. But there are so many brands out there, that I advise you to TASTE your marinade before you use it. You can then judge its heat level and add a dash of hot sauce if you like. And it will help you decide whether or not to use the chilli in the salsa.

For a picture of this dish, see page 90

BIBLIOGRAPHY

American Bar, Charles Schumann, 1995
Casino Royale, Ian Fleming, 1953
Cocktails: How To Mix Them, Robert Vermeire, 1922
Cosmopolitan: A Bartender's Life, Toby Cecchini, 2004
Harry's ABC of Mixing Cocktails, Harry MacElhone, 1922
The Savoy Cocktail Book, Harry Craddock, 1930

'Just Another Tequila Sunrise' by Jeff Burkhart, National Geographic Assignment blog (ngablog.com), 17 February 2012

FILMOGRAPHY

The Big Sleep (Howard Hawks, 1946)
Blue Hawaii (Norman Taurog, 1961)
Casablanca (Michael Curtiz, 1942)
Casino Royale (Martin Campbell, 2006)
South Pacific (Joshua Logan, 1958)
Teacher's Pet (George Seaton, 1958)
The Thin Man (W.S. Van Dyke, 1934)

Mad Men (TV series created by Matthew Weiner), first aired 2007

Fine and Dandy (musical by Kay Swift), first produced on Broadway in 1930

INDEX

First published in 2014 by Mitchell Beazley,
a part of Octopus Publishing Group,
Endeavour House, 189 Shaftesbury Avenue,
London WC2H 8JY
www.octopusbooks.co.uk

An Hachette UK Company
www.hachette.co.uk

British Library Cataloguing-in-Publication Data.
A catalogue record for this book is available from
the British Library.

Publisher: **Alison Starling**

Editor: **Alex Stetter**

Design: **Juliette Norsworthy**

Photography: **Kate Whitaker**

Illustrations: **Abigail Read**

Assistant Production Manager: **Caroline Alberti**

ISBN 978 1 84533 881 7

Printed & bound in China

Author's acknowledgements

First, a huge thanks to Alison Starling, Juliette Norsworthy,
Alex Stetter, The Governess (aka Denise Bates) – quite simply
the best publishing team ever.

Thank you to Kate and her glamourous assistant Badger
for the beautiful pictures, to Abi for illustrations which look
as though she's seen the inside of my head and captured
everything I imagined, and to Liz Belton.

Many thanks too to my brilliant contributors for allowing
me to use their recipes: in order of appearance, James Bond
and the Fleming Estate for allowing my quotations from *Casino
Royale*; Tom Williams; Ian Kittichai and Sarah Chang and
the team at Hyde & Seek, Bangkok; Chris van Hoy and Julia
Travis at Kin Shop, Manhattan; Michel Dozois; Bricia Lopez and
Guelaguetza, Los Angeles; Luca Missaglia, Jeremy Lee and
Eddie and Sam Hart at Quo Vadis, London; Jarret Wrisley at
Soul Food Mahanakorn, Bangkok; Julian Cox, Ricardo Zarate,
Stephane Bombet and the team at Picca, Los Angeles; Vince
and Jen Jung at my beloved Formosa Café, Los Angeles; Khun
Sompong and his successors at the Oriental Hotel's Bamboo
Bar, Bangkok; Mark Hix and team at The Fish and Oyster House,
Lyme Regis; Nick Cuthbert; and Khun Jao Fa and all at the
Tamarind Village Hotel, Chiang Mai.

You can't cook much without some jolly good suppliers, so
I also want to thank Chris, Clarence and the team at The
Parson's Nose, Putney; Dodie at the Cool Chile Company;
Luis and Oscar at MexiTrade; Donna and Geoff at Chang
Beer for the Mekhong and SangSom; The Barnes Fish Shop;
Gerry's Wine and Spirits, from whom you can buy just about
anything; The Whisky Exchange for turning deliveries around
at an impossible rate; KitchenAid for such marvellous gadgetry
and Joe Keeper at Bar Keeper, Los Angeles, for glasses and
barware extraordinaire.

And finally my lovely and hugely supportive family; my chic
and lovely agents Felicity Blunt and Jo Wander; the fragrant
Lindsay Stewart at Fab Communications, the Octopi, who were
subjected to an evening of cocktails and canapés at Alison's
instigation and a morning of Alka Seltzer at their own; Alison
Kwee at Wagstaff Worldwide; Jo Harris at Hix; Claudine Triolo
at Tamarind Village; Jessica Smith at Ann Scott Associates;
and last but not least, Freddie – just look where an evening of
martinis got us all those years ago!!!